THE 8-H PRINCIPLE

For Success at Work and Life

KAUSHIK GHOSH

Om Books International

First published in 2024 by

Om Books International

Corporate & Editorial Office
A-12, Sector 64, Noida 201 301
Uttar Pradesh, India
Phone: +91 120 477 4100
Email: editorial@ombooks.com
Website: www.ombooksinternational.com

Sales Office
107, Ansari Road, Darya Ganj,
New Delhi 110 002, India
Phone: +91 11 4000 9000
Email: sales@ombooks.com
Website: www.ombooks.com

Copyright © Kaushik Ghosh 2024

ALL RIGHTS RESERVED. The views and opinions expressed in this book are those of the author, and have been verified to the extent possible, and the publishers are in no way liable for the same. No part of this book may be reproduced or transmitted in any form by any means, electronic or mechanical, including photocopying and recording, or by any information storage and retrieval system, except as may be expressly permitted in writing by the publisher.

ISBN: 978-93-5376-978-9

Printed in India

10 9 8 7 6 5 4 3 2 1

Kaushik Ghosh, a wanderer at heart, is a maestro orchestrating the symphony of life, blending eloquence, passion and the insatiable desire to explore the uncharted realms of human experience.

A confluence of roles adorns Kaushik—a traveller who aims to travel all the countries around the world, an orator, a lifestyle coach, a presenter, a radio jockey, a passionate photographer. Born of the cultural cradle of Kolkata, a proud alumnus of Frank Anthony Public School and Scottish Church College, Kaushik embodies the spirit of the city that breathes life into dreams.

In October 2022, he unfurled his literary wings with *Man of the Match—Life of a Common Man*, a Bengali memoir that unravels the tapestry of his journey from the innocence of childhood to the challenges of the first job. The pages dance with nostalgia, humour and wisdom inviting readers into the inner sanctum of his experience.

As Chief Operating Officer of a prominent Indian corporation, Kaushik Ghosh has scaled professional summits, but his heart remains tethered to the extraordinary stories woven by seemingly ordinary people. His third literary endeavour, currently in the making, promises to be an inspiration, showcasing the remarkable feats of those who often dwell in the shadows.

As he continues to pen his chapters of success, we eagerly anticipate the stories he will unfold and the worlds he will traverse, inspiring us all to embrace the extraordinary within the ordinary.

Praise for the Book

"Within the pages of this insightful book, the author unveils the impactful 8-H Principle for success at work and life, a guiding framework that left an indelible mark on my perspective. As I immersed myself in its teachings, a clear message emerged—illuminating the intrinsic purpose of our existence: to contribute positively to the lives of others. Before encountering this profound work, I had never fully appreciated the simple act of breathing. Now, with newfound awareness, each breath becomes a conscious acknowledgment of the precious gift of life. I am compelled to ensure that this gift is not idly wasted. Gratitude has become a daily practice, with a sincere thankfulness to the Almighty for the privilege of being alive and the commitment to being of genuine use to everyone I encounter, be it in the realm of my professional endeavours or within the broader tapestry of society. This book has not only altered my perspective, but also sparked a transformative journey towards a purposeful and grateful existence."

—**Subhasish Chakraborty**, founder and chairman, DTDC

'Kaushik Ghosh brings us back to what truly matters. *The 8-H Principle* is profound, thought-provoking and a great reminder of revisiting our conscience."

—**Noopur Desai**, chief of global business network, Nishith Desai Associates

"Kaushik Ghosh's book makes for a wonderful and inspirational read to help navigate our life and work."

—**Anupam Roy**, singer, lyricist, composer

"In today's world, when everybody is busy with so many things happening around them and nobody has the time to look back and take a deep breath, Kaushik Ghosh has provided a fresh perspective on life. Just sit back and read a few lines to know how to approach life and work, and enjoy the greatest wealth God has given—'being human'. Delighted to read the principles articulated which make me think that I have wasted the most valuable treasure of my life: time."

—**Naresh Jalan**, managing director, Ramkrishna Forgings Limited

"This book is a life lesson. By using what he calls the 8-H Principle, Kaushik Ghosh articulates some basic fundamentals of happy living that we so often overlook and tend to take for granted. Using his own life story, this book is a timely reminder of what we stand for and we need to do to live a fulfilled life. Well written in lucid prose, this book could be a management tool for any aspiring student."

—**Boria Majumdar**, sports historian and journalist, co-writer of Sachin Tendulkar's autobiography *Playing It My Way*.

Contents

Preface ix

Introduction xv
The Foundations of a Meaningful Life

1. Honesty 1

2. Hard Work 27

3. Hobby 59

4. Holiday 81

5. Health 111

6. Humility 147

7. Humanity 167

8. Hope 197

Conclusion 215

Preface

On the morning of 28 March 2023, as the golden rays of the sun caressed the emerald hill station, Nature seemed to dance in harmony with our joyous spirits. For days, grey clouds had veiled the azure canvas, teasing us with intermittent showers. But now, the heavens unveiled a majestic display of cerulean splendour, blessed by the warmth of a benevolent sun. Amid this picturesque serenity, nestled among verdant tea plantations and majestic mountain ranges, our merry band of seventeen revelled in the bliss of our vacation.

After a scrumptious breakfast, we embarked on a spirited game of cricket, each swing of the bat resounding with echoes of laughter and camaraderie. Our spirits were soaring higher than the lofty peaks, as we basked in the radiance of this sublime moment.

Yet, destiny had a twist in its tale, a fickle turn completely unforeseen. An unexpected intruder, invisible but insidious, suddenly seized me. Like a bolt of lightning, pain coursed through the very fabric of my being. I trembled and convulsed in its merciless grip. The pleasant sound of laughter was abruptly silenced, replaced by gasps of concern and anxious whispers.

As the ache pulsated through my veins, the world around me blurred. Time seemed suspended, as if Nature herself held her breath in anticipation of the unknown. The sky, once a canopy of pure serenity, now bore witness to the vulnerability of mortal existence. Through my agony, I glimpsed the transient nature of human existence, a reminder that even amid the most idyllic settings, life's capricious currents can steer us into turbulent waters. Yet, even in this violent storm of pain, a faint flicker of hope endured—that of resilience and the triumph of the human spirit.

At first, I believed it to be a mere case of acidity, a fleeting discomfort that could be subdued with a simple pill. However, as time passed, the pain began to swell within me. My body shook with each breath and beads of sweat trickled down my forehead. I knew with a deepening sense of dread that something was gravely wrong. I finally had to acknowledge the urgent need for medical intervention.

To get an ECG done, I would have to drive down to the only local hospital in the heart of the city. So I quickly embarked on that treacherous journey, a race against fate. As I arrived at the hospital, I was met with the devastating news that the doctor who could help me had left for the day. But a kind-hearted local directed me to a nearby medical shop, a sanctuary amid the turmoil. With trembling hands and a fearful heart, I made my way down the narrow hilly road to Krishna Medical Shop.

There, I met the compassionate owner. Seeing me in agony, he sprang into action, calling upon the person who could perform the ECG. Within moments, the saviour arrived, and I underwent the test. My world stood still as the results emerged. The ECG machine revealed a sombre truth, confirming my unspoken fear—the onslaught of a heart attack.

The situation was dire, and I knew that I needed to act fast in order to survive. My doctor friend had arranged everything, but we were in a remote location, far away from the nearest hospital. I had to be transported to Siliguri, where the operation could be performed. But time was of the essence.

As I further made my way down the hill, a long one-and-a-half-hour journey, my vitality waned. It felt as if I was stumbling through the valley of mortality or walking a tenuous tightrope strung high above the eternal abyss. The last thirty minutes were nothing short of harrowing, as every second felt like an eternity, and the fear of death lingered heavily in the air. The sheer fragility of life, often blurred by the hustle and bustle of our dailiness, was now thrust into sharp focus—how fragile our grip on existence truly is!

As the minutes ticked by, each seeming more treacherous than the last, a profound reflection washed over me. Memories and thoughts of the past, present and future swirled around like a tempest. I reflected on the choices I had made and the paths I had taken, wondering if I had lived my life to its fullest potential. Regret mingled with hope, as I thought of all the dreams I still wanted to chase, the adventures I still wanted to embark on and the people I still wanted to meet. The realization hit me like a thunderbolt—there was still so much left to experience, so much left to see and so much left to do … I could not bear the thought of leaving this world without having lived a life full of passion and purpose, without having left my mark on the world in some small way.

In that surreal moment, I was reminded that each moment we are given is a precious gift, not to be squandered or taken for granted. It was a humbling experience, one that left me with a newfound appreciation for every breath I take, and a burning desire to make each one count. I made a promise to myself that if I survived this ordeal, I would live each day with purpose and intention, making the most of every opportunity that came my way.

As I entered the hospital, the mere thought that I might not survive the surgery was enough to chill me to the bone. But as I lay on the operating table, surrounded by a team of medical professionals, I felt an unexpected sense of calm. And when I emerged from the surgery, dazed and disoriented, I knew that I had been given a second chance at life.

No longer shackled by anxiety or stress, I appeared with a radiant countenance, aglow with immense gratitude. The very act of drawing breath took on a newfound profundity—a melody of life sang through every fibre of my being. The fragility of existence, once a distant notion, wrapped my heart in a tender embrace now. The trivialities of yesteryears melted away, replaced by an ardent desire to seize each precious moment and paint my existence with vibrant hues. Henceforth, my existence became a testament to the resilience of the human spirit, which, once dormant, had now awoken in me.

Our time on this earth is limited. And yet, we often choose to turn a blind eye to this inevitability and live as if we are immortal. But when we grasp the reality of our own mortality, something magical happens. We begin to see life with new eyes, gaze upon its kaleidoscope of wonders as if for the first time and savour each moment with the appreciation of how precious time is. Within this realization, lie the seeds of profound wisdom and liberation.

With every heartbeat, we stand at the threshold of creation, armed with the brush of intention and the palette of dreams. Death's inevitability compels us to wield these tools with grace, to paint upon the tapestry of our days the colours of joy and wonder. We cast aside daily trivialities and embark on the grand pilgrimage of purpose, driven by the yearning to leave footprints upon the shores of time. In this pursuit, our dreams become our compass, guiding us through the labyrinth of uncertainty as we unravel the mysteries of our potential.

Meeting mortality's solemn gaze, we are reminded that survival is the most fundamental thing in human life. It is the foundation upon which we build our hopes, our dreams, our aspirations. Survival is the basic instinct that drives us to seek food, shelter, safety. And when our basic needs are met, we contemplate more complex and meaningful pursuits.

And yet, survival alone is not enough. We must imbue our existence with a resolute determination to make a difference in the world. Our purpose is what gives us a sense of direction and helps us make choices that align with our values and goals.

Furthermore, it is in giving that we truly fulfil our purpose in life. To help others, to uplift and inspire, to create something beautiful and enduring—these are the things that bestow meaning upon our existence. After all, in the end, what truly matters is not the number of years we live but the impact we make on the world.

The culmination of all these elements is a fulfilling life. Fulfilment does not reside in the material possessions we amass, nor is it measured by the heights we ascend in our careers. Instead, it resides in the intangible—the way we touch the lives of others and the strength with which we embrace our purpose. It is a state of being in which we awaken each day with a sense of anticipation, knowing that our existence holds significance and purpose.

When we can survive, pursue our purpose and make a difference in the lives of others, we experience a sense of wholeness and satisfaction that is unparalleled. If we focus on survival at the expense of our purpose, we find ourselves feeling empty and unfulfilled. Similarly, if we pursue our purpose without considering the needs of others, we find ourselves feeling isolated and disconnected. Ultimately, a fulfilling life is about finding a balance between these elements. Embrace survival with gratitude, for it provides the canvas upon which purpose can be painted. We should allow purpose to guide our steps, illuminating the path and propelling us towards self-actualization. And in the spirit of giving, let our compassion flow like a river, nurturing.

But the fulfilment we seek is not a mere destination, a single summit to conquer. Rather, it is a constant dance of authenticity, where our footsteps align with the rhythm of our souls. In this dance of survival, purpose and giving, we cease to be merely spectators or passive observers of our existence. Instead, we become active participants in the grand drama of life.

With each step we take, guided by the light of our purpose, let us contribute to the collective symphony. In this pursuit, we shall discover a life complete, an opus of beauty and meaning that echoes through eternity. This book is a step in that direction.

Introduction

The Foundations of a Meaningful Life

Do you ever feel like you are spinning your wheels and not making any progress towards your goals? It can be frustrating and demotivating, but there is a solution: what I choose to call the 8-H Principle—a set of values that can help us lead a purposeful life. The principle focuses on cultivating a holistic approach to life, emphasizing the importance of both physical and mental health, as well as personal and professional growth. The 8-H Principle will help you build stronger relationships and achieve your goals and, most importantly, live a happy and fulfilling life.

In this book, we will delve into each of these principles. But before we do so, we must understand and appreciate the very foundations of life. What is the innate instinct that drives us all? How do we add meaning to life? What is our purpose? What is constant in our lives? And what do we gain by giving? Let us explore these ideas and discover marvellous joys as we prepare to embark on our journey towards leading a truly meaningful life.

Survival

> "Survival can be summed up in three words, never give up. That's the heart of it really. Just keep trying."—Bear Grylls

Survival is the primal instinct that drives us all. It is the beating heart of our existence, the source of our strength and the reason for our resilience. Every living organism, from the smallest microbe to the biggest of beasts, is imbued with an instinct to survive. It is an urge that drives them to seek out food, water, shelter and safety at all costs.

For millions of years, life on this planet has been a constant battle for survival. Our bodies, honed by millennia of evolution, are finely tuned machines capable of incredible feats of endurance and resilience.

Whether it is a life-threatening illness or a close brush with death, the realization that our time on this earth is finite can be both humbling and empowering. It forces us to confront the fragility of our existence and makes us realize the importance of survival. Without survival, there would be no life, no love, no joy, no art, no beauty. It is the starting point of all things, the bedrock upon which we build our lives.

Survival as the foundation of everything

Consider, for a moment, the miracle of existence itself. The unfathomable odds that led to the creation of the universe, our planet and the myriad life forms that have since arisen to populate it. We are here because our ancestors survived. They fought, they adapted, they overcame. And so, we carry within us the legacy of their triumphs.

But survival is not just a matter of physical endurance. It encompasses every aspect of our being, from the biological to the psychological, from the emotional to the spiritual. We survive not just to sustain our bodies but to feed our souls. We strive not just to stay alive but to find meaning and purpose in our existence. It is about creating something that will endure beyond our mortal lives. Therefore, in many ways, the struggle for survival is the ultimate expression of human creativity.

The struggle for survival is what connects us all, no matter where we come from or what our individual experiences may be. It is the reason we can empathize with others, understand their struggles, and offer support and compassion when it is needed the most.

Then let us embrace survival fully. For it is in the struggle for survival that we find our truest selves, our greatest strengths and our most profound connections with the world around us.

Survival as responsibility

In October 1972, a Uruguayan rugby team—a total of forty-five people, including players, their family members and friends as well as the crew—set off on a plane to Chile for a rugby match. However, it crashed into the Andes Mountains, leaving the survivors stranded in one of the harshest environments on earth. Twenty-nine people were dead instantly and another eight succumbed to their injuries soon after. And the survivors were left with no food, no medical supplies and limited clothing in the freezing temperatures.

As days passed, the survivors resorted to eating whatever they could find from the plane's wreckage. They hoped for rescue, but none came. The situation became more dire when an avalanche hit their makeshift shelter, killing many of them and destroying much of what was left of the plane. Realizing that they might never be rescued, Nando Parrado, a member of the rugby team, and another survivor, Roberto Canessa, decided to make a dangerous trek through the mountains to seek help. They embarked on a journey that took them ten days, during which they had to climb over a mountain pass and wade through deep snowdrifts. On the tenth day, Parrado and Canessa finally stumbled upon a group of shepherds, who then informed authorities and led a rescue team to the survivors. After seventy-two days in the mountains, the sixteen survivors were finally rescued.

The survivors became famous for their incredible feat of perseverance and survival. It was later recounted in Piers Paul Read's book *Alive* and in the movie adaptation of the same name. Parrado has since become a motivational speaker and has written a book about his experiences called *Miracle in the Andes: 72 Days on the Mountain and My Long Trek Home*.

Survival is not just a personal goal, it is also a responsibility. We are all responsible for our own survival, so we must take care of ourselves, both physically and emotionally, and be proactive in our efforts to stay alive. This means eating healthy, exercising regularly, managing stress and seeking help when needed. When we prioritize our survival, we are also taking care of our loved ones, our communities and the world at large.

In the face of adversity, it can be tempting to look for someone else to blame or to rely on others to solve our problems, but it is up to each individual to take control of their own destiny and to chart their own course. It is not always easy, and there are bound to be setbacks and failures along the way. And it is in these moments that we rise above ourselves and prove our strength. As the poet William Ernest Henley wrote, "I am the master of my fate / I am the captain of my soul."

Survival as a mindset

Survival is not just a physical feat, it is also a state of mind—a way of thinking that allows us to overcome even the most daunting of obstacles. It is the ability to stay calm under pressure, think critically, adapt to changing circumstances and never give up. It is the will to keep going when all seems lost, the determination to rise after every setback and the unwavering belief that we can achieve anything we set our minds to.

To truly understand the power of the survival mindset, one must look no further than the natural world. Take, for example, the salmon, which swims upstream against strong currents and overcomes numerous other obstacles to reach its breeding ground. It never loses its sense of purpose or determination.

Or take the humble octopus. It can squeeze through impossibly small spaces and even detach its arm to escape a predator. It is this kind of adaptability that makes the octopus a survivor.

Coming to the human realm, the story of Aron Ralston is worth recalling. In 2003, Ralston was hiking alone in Utah when a boulder fell on his arm, trapping him in a narrow canyon. After five days of being stuck, with limited food and water, Ralston amputated his arm. He used a pocketknife to sever his arm below the elbow, then rappelled down a 65-foot wall and hiked out of the canyon to safety. This was not simply an act of desperation, but a display of the survival mindset, which enabled him to push past pain and fear to save his life.

But survival is not a quality restricted to extraordinary people. It can be found in ordinary people: a single mother who works two jobs to provide for her children or the student who overcomes a learning disability to graduate with honours. These are people who have developed the survival mindset and who refuse to be defeated by the challenges they face.

Survival as an essential for helping others

Imagine you are on an aeroplane and the oxygen masks suddenly drop down. The instructions are clear: put your own mask on before helping others. Why? Because if you do not secure your own supply of oxygen, you will not be able to help anyone else to do the same. This simple practice is a powerful reminder of the importance of self-preservation in any situation.

Take, for example, the story of the *Titanic*. When the ship hit an iceberg and began to sink, people were scrambling to get onto lifeboats. But in the midst of the chaos, there were heroes like Molly Brown, who not only survived but also rescued others by taking control of a lifeboat. If she had not ensured her own survival, she would not have been able to help as many people as she did.

The act of survival itself can be a powerful motivator for altruistic behaviour. When we face difficult circumstances, such as illness, poverty, or persecution, we often develop a heightened sense of empathy and compassion for others who are experiencing similar hardships. This shared experience can inspire us to work towards collective survival.

This idea is also reflected in many cultural traditions and myths. In Greek mythology, the hero Theseus must survive a series of trials to ultimately defeat the Minotaur and save his people. Similarly, in many Native American cultures, the hero must first undergo a journey of self-discovery before he is able to help his community.

Thus, survival is not a selfish goal. In reality, survival is a prerequisite for helping others. Taking care of your own self is not a luxury, but a duty.

As the poet John Donne wrote, "No man is an island, entire of itself; every man / Is a piece of the continent, a part of the main." We must recognize our own value as a part of the larger whole and prioritize our survival as a means of contributing to the survival of all.

We must survive also for those who depend on us. Whether it is our family, friends or colleagues, we have a responsibility to them, and we must do everything in our power to ensure that we are there for them when they need us.

Purpose

What is the meaning of life? This is a question that has been pondered for centuries by philosophers, scientists, and people like you and me. It has no right answer and is open to interpretation. Some people believe that the meaning of life lies in seeking happiness, while others believe it lies in fulfilling a higher purpose. At its core, the meaning of life is subjective and personal and can be shaped by a variety of factors. What gives meaning to one person's life may not give meaning to another's.

Therefore, let us talk about the meaning of life that has to do with finding a sense of direction and purpose, and living in accordance with our values and beliefs.

One of the key aspects of a meaningful life is personal growth and self-actualization. This involves pursuing our passions and interests, learning new skills and striving to be the best version of ourselves. Humans are social creatures, and our connections with others play a significant role in our sense of purpose and well-being. Cultivating healthy relationships with family, friends and community can bring joy, support and a sense of belonging to our lives.

Service to others is also an important aspect of a meaningful life. Helping those in need and contributing to the greater good— whether through volunteering, donating to charity or simply being kind to those around us—can make a significant impact on others as well as on ourselves. Spirituality can also contribute towards the same. For some, this may mean practising a particular religion or belief system, while for others, it may involve a deeper association with Nature or a sense of interconnectedness with all living beings.

Therefore, by focusing on cultivating positive relationships, personal growth, service to others and a sense of spirituality or connection to something greater, we can create a more meaningful and fulfilling life for ourselves and those around us.

How to add purpose to your life

While the meaningful life varies from one person to the next, one common theme persists—the meaning of life lies in a search for purpose. This search can be seen as an innate drive that is present in us, regardless of culture or background. Living a purposeful life is a common aspiration for many people, but finding one's purpose in life can be a daunting task. Let me outline some tips that have helped me in my journey.

Define your purpose

Take time to reflect on what is important to you and what you want to achieve in life. Is it personal growth? Achieving a specific goal? Learning new skills? Or experiencing new cultures? Having a clear sense of purpose will help guide your decisions and actions.

Ask yourself what you want your legacy to be

How do you want to be remembered when you are no longer there? What impact do you want to have on the world?

Set S-M-A-R-T goals

Once you have identified your values, passions and purpose, set concrete goals that align with them. Goals will help you stay motivated. Make sure your goals are **s**pecific, **m**easurable, **a**chievable, **r**elevant and **t**ime-bound (S-M-A-R-T).

Focus on the present

Instead of worrying about the future or dwelling on the past, focus on the present moment. This will help you fully experience and appreciate your life's journey and make the most of the opportunities that come your way.

Embrace new experiences

Step out of your comfort zone and try new things. Also, be open to new perspectives and ideas. This will help you learn and grow and create memories that will last a lifetime.

Connect with others

Take time to get to know people and learn from their experiences. Build relationships and connect with people. This will create a fulfilling sense of community.

Practise gratitude

Pause to appreciate the small things in life and express gratitude for everything that comes your way. This will help you maintain a positive mindset in your journey.

Learn from challenges

Challenges and obstacles are a part of any journey. Instead of getting discouraged, look for opportunities to learn and grow from these experiences.

Cultivate positive habits

Habits such as regular exercise, reading and journaling can help you stay focused, reduce stress and improve your overall well-being.

Volunteer or give back to the community

Help others, which will give you a sense of accomplishment and fulfilment. It will also connect you with like-minded individuals.

Meditate

Connect with your inner self and gain clarity on what truly matters to you. Meditation will also help you reduce stress and anxiety.

Seek feedback

Ask trusted friends or family members to share what they see as your strengths and passions. Sometimes others can see things in us that we are simply unable to see in ourselves.

Remember that life is a journey, not a destination. Therefore, you need to be patient and open to new experiences, and you may find that your purpose evolves over time. You just need to ensure that you are not short of intent and are focused directionally.

Discover the power of intent and direction

In the early hours of one morning, while walking along a beach, I noticed a group of small fish that had come ashore with the ocean water and gotten stranded. I watched as they struggled to breathe and survive out of the water. I felt a sudden urge to do something to help these creatures, and so I decided to throw one of them back into the water to give it a chance to survive. Picking up one of the fish and holding it in my hand, I realized how fragile and vulnerable these creatures were. I gently put it back into the water and watched as it swam away with renewed energy. Although it was just one fish, it felt like a small victory. I felt a sense of satisfaction and joy knowing that I had made a difference in the life of that little organism.

This experience made me reflect on the power of direction and intent. It is not about the size of the action or the number of lives saved, but rather the intention behind it. It is easy to get caught up in the hustle and bustle of our daily lives and forget about the little things that matter—small gestures and actions. But the truth is that every action counts, no matter how small, for even the smallest act of kindness can have a profound impact on the world around us.

What do we mean by direction? It simply refers to the path we choose to follow in life, which involves setting goals and working towards achieving them. It is essential to have a clear direction in life, as it helps us focus our efforts and energy on the things that matter most to us. Intent, on the other hand, refers to the underlying motivations and values that drive our actions. Our intent is what inspires us to pursue our goals and guides us in making the right decisions. It is the foundation of our character and shapes our perspective on life. When we combine a clear direction with good intent, we create a powerful force that can positively impact the lives of others.

Embrace change: The key to finding happiness

In today's fast-paced society, it is easy to get bogged down in the daily grind of our jobs and responsibilities. The repetitive tasks we undertake each day can leave us feeling uninspired and unfulfilled. Hence, seeking meaning in life and adding a purpose to it is crucial to our happiness and overall well-being. And this can only be achieved if we are open to embracing change.

Change is a constant and an inevitable aspect of our lives. The seasons come and go, the tides rise and fall, and the stars in the sky move across the horizon. Even the cells in our bodies constantly undergo change and renewal. Change can manifest in various forms. It can be sudden and unexpected, such as a job loss or a health crisis, or it can be gradual and planned, such as moving to a new city or getting married. Change can also be positive or negative, depending on our perspective and how we respond to it.

Why do we resist change?

Change is inevitable, yet many of us find it challenging to accept and cope with it. If we resist it, we deprive ourselves of the potential for growth and happiness. Those who seize new opportunities and experiences are more resilient and better equipped to navigate the challenges that come their way. The ability to adapt to change is thus a skill that is vital for success and fulfilment in life. But why do we resist change, to begin with?

Fear of the unknown: It is no surprise that the familiar feels safe and predictable, while the unknown feels risky and uncertain. We may worry that change will disrupt our lives too much and that we will lose control or will not be able to adapt to new circumstances. To overcome this fear, we need to learn to embrace the unknown and focus on the potential benefits of the change rather than the risks. We can also remind ourselves that we have successfully adapted to changes in the past and that we have the skills and resources to do so again.

Loss of comfort and familiarity: We have established routines, habits and relationships that make us feel secure, and change threatens to disrupt these patterns. But we need to recognize that growth and progress often require us to step out of those comfort zones.

Fear of failure: Change involves taking risks and trying new things, and we may worry that we will not succeed. We also worry about what others will think if we fail. Yet, it is essential to understand that failure is a natural part of the learning process. Also, failure is not a reflection of our worth as a person, for we can learn from our mistakes and use them as opportunities to grow and improve.

Lack of trust in the process of change: We may not trust the very process of change or the people driving it. Or perhaps the change is not well thought out or it will not be implemented properly. It may even be that the change is forced upon us without our input or feedback. But we can build trust in the process by seeking out information about it, asking questions and giving feedback, even offering our support and expertise.

How to embrace change?

In choosing to embrace change, we turn uncertainty into opportunity. By stepping outside our comfort zone, we can discover new passions and talents that we never knew we had. By being open to new experiences, we can find joy and meaning in our lives, and purpose and fulfilment in it. With the right mindset and approach, we can turn challenges into opportunities for growth. Here are some tips that can help you embrace change.

Practice mindfulness: Be present in the moment without judgement or distraction. By cultivating mindfulness, we can learn to accept the present as it is, rather than constantly striving for something else. This will help us feel more comfortable with change, as we learn to let go of our attachment to the past or the future.

Focus on the positive: Instead of seeing change as a threat or risk, try viewing it as an opportunity. Ask yourself: What can I learn from this experience? Or, how can this change help me grow? In simple words, instead of dwelling on the potential negative outcomes of a change, focus on the positives.

Take small steps: Change can be overwhelming, especially if we try to tackle too much at once. Instead, we should try taking small steps towards the change we want to make. We need to break it down into manageable pieces and celebrate each small success along the way. This will help build momentum and confidence, and make the change feel less daunting.

Seek support: Change can be difficult to navigate alone hence seek support from friends, family or a therapist. Having someone to talk to can help us process our emotions and gain perspective as well as provide encouragement and accountability as we work towards our goals.

Be patient: Change does not happen overnight, so it is important to be patient with ourselves and give the process of change time to mature and come to fruition.

In the end, embracing change requires courage, flexibility and a willingness to let go of the familiar to explore the new.

Different responses to change

Steve Jobs is known for his role in revolutionizing the technology industry and transforming multiple industries, including music, personal computing and mobile phones. In the early 1980s, Jobs was a young entrepreneur who had already experienced both success and failure. After co-founding Apple with Steve Wozniak, he helped create the Apple Macintosh, which achieved significant success. However, due to conflicts within the company, Jobs was eventually ousted from Apple in 1985. This event marked a significant turning point in his life and career. Rather than letting it define him, Jobs chose to embrace change and start a new chapter in his life.

After leaving Apple, Jobs founded NeXT Computer, a company focused on developing high-end computers for the education and business sectors. Although NeXT faced numerous challenges and struggled to gain market traction, Jobs persisted and remained passionate about his vision for innovation. In 1996, Apple was facing its own struggles and was in desperate need of fresh ideas. Recognizing the need for change, Apple acquired NeXT, bringing Steve Jobs back into the company. This move set the stage for an incredible transformation.

Jobs took over as interim CEO of Apple and initiated a series of bold changes. Under his leadership, Apple introduced groundbreaking products such as the iMac, iPod, iPhone and iPad. These transformations propelled Apple from the brink of bankruptcy to one of the most valuable and influential companies in the world. Jobs' unwavering commitment to embracing change and his ability to envision the future transformed not only his own life, but also the lives of millions of people worldwide.

Now, a different story. In the 1970s and 80s, Kodak was a dominant player in the photography market, a household name. In 1996, it had a 27 per cent share in the film market and a market capitalization of $31 billion. However, the digital revolution in photography was gaining momentum, and Kodak's failure to adapt to it proved to be disastrous. In the early 2000s, the company's revenues and profits began to decline rapidly as consumers shifted to digital cameras and stopped buying film. Kodak tried to catch up by launching its own digital camera, but it was too little, too late. The company's share in the film market plummeted to 7 per cent, and its market capitalization fell to less than $3 billion.

Kodak filed for bankruptcy in 2012 and had to sell off most of its patents to stay afloat. The failure to embrace change and adjust to the new digital era at the right time led to the downfall of one of the most iconic companies.

While Steve Jobs' story is a testament to the power of embracing change, Kodak's is precisely the opposite. The world is constantly evolving, hence businesses and individuals must be willing to evolve to stay relevant and successful.

The Covid-19 pandemic has been one of the most significant disruptions of our time, forcing us to rethink our ways of life and the way we work. People have had to learn new skills, unlearn old ones and adapt to the new reality to stay afloat. The pandemic has highlighted the importance of being agile, flexible and willing to learn new things to succeed in the ever-changing world.

In this challenging environment, businesses that embraced technology and adapted to the new normal were able to survive and even thrive. For example, restaurants that quickly shifted to online ordering and delivery services have been able to maintain and expand their customer base and stay open. In contrast, restaurants that refused to change their operations have been forced to close.

Furthermore, there was a sudden shift to the concept of remote work. Many people had to quickly adapt to working from home, often in less-than-ideal conditions. This required new skills such as effective time management, communication and collaboration. The education sector was also deeply impacted. With most schools and universities closed, students had to adapt to online learning. In both cases, those able to master the required skills were able to continue their work or studies uninterrupted, while others fell behind, many even losing their jobs.

Overall, the pandemic highlighted the importance of digital skills. Many companies are now looking for people with specific digital marketing skills to help them transition to online sales. Those who have these skills have been able to find job opportunities, but others have struggled to find employment. The Covid-19 pandemic has been a wake-up call for all of us. It has shown us that change is inevitable, and those who embrace it are the ones who thrive.

Change and spirituality: The Bhagavad Gita

The Bhagavad Gita has influenced many great thinkers and spiritual leaders throughout history. More than anything else, it is a comprehensive guide to living a fulfilling life, and one of its central themes is accepting change. The Gita emphasizes that everything in life is impermanent—not only physical objects but also emotions, thoughts and beliefs. In fact, the only constant in life is change, and therefore, it is important to accept and embrace it.

In one of the most celebrated passages in the Gita, Lord Krishna advises Arjuna on the battlefield of Kurukshetra: "The wise lament neither for the living nor for the dead. There was never a time when I did not exist, nor you, nor any of these kings; nor is there any future in which we shall cease to be (Chapter 2, Verses 11–12)." This passage reminds us that we are all part of the eternal, unchanging consciousness that pervades the universe. Our bodies and our circumstances may change, but our true nature remains constant.

The concept of karma is another important teaching in the Gita. Our actions have consequences, and we must accept the results of our actions. This means that if we want to change our circumstances, we must change our actions. The Gita also emphasizes that our actions must be selfless and performed with detachment from the outcome. Hence, we should focus on doing what is right and not worry about the consequences. By doing so, we can create positive change in our lives and in the world around us.

Change can be difficult and painful, the Gita reminds us, yet it is necessary for growth. Lord Krishna tells Arjuna, "The pleasures that arise from contact with the senses are the sources of all suffering, and they come and go like the winter and summer seasons. They arise from the senses, and one must learn to tolerate them without being disturbed" (Chapter 2, Verse 14). From this passage, we know how important it is to accept the ups and downs of life without being attached to them. By doing so, we can develop the strength and resilience to face the challenges that come our way.

By understanding the impermanence of all things, we can focus on what is truly important. The Gita's teachings on karma and detachment remind us that we have the power to change our circumstances, but we must do so with selflessness and a focus on doing what is right. These lessons on change are as relevant today as they were thousands of years ago.

Giving

> "We make a living by what we get, but we make a life by what we give."—Winston Churchill

Giving is the most giving. This is a profound truth that has been repeated through the ages and for good reason. There is a certain magic in the act of giving, a transformative power that can change the lives of both the giver and the receiver.

Giving is an art, a masterpiece painted with the colours of kindness and compassion. It is a selfless act, an offering of oneself to the world, a reflection of the beauty and grace that resides within us. Indeed, giving brings us closer to our own humanity and to the divine spark that animates us all.

At its core, giving is an act of love. When we give, we express our love for others, for the world and for ourselves. By sharing our abundance with those in need, we make a difference in their lives, and in turn, in the world. It is a way of showing that we care and that we are willing to put the needs of others before our own. And in doing so, we create a ripple effect of kindness and compassion that can spread far beyond the initial act of giving.

Take, for example, the story of a man named Jonny Benjamin. At the age of twenty, he was diagnosed with schizophrenia and was struggling to cope with his illness. One day, Jonny decided to take his own life by jumping off a bridge. But a stranger intervened, talking him down from the edge and saving his life. Years later, Jonny set out on a mission to find and thank the stranger who had saved him. With the help of social media, he was able to track down the man, Neil Laybourn. And in a beautiful act of gratitude, Jonny decided to run the London Marathon with Neil.

Their journey together was captured in a heart-warming video that went viral, as well as a documentary titled *The Stranger on the Bridge*, inspiring millions of people around the world. In the end, what started as an instinctive act of kindness—one stranger saving another—became a powerful reminder of the transformative power of giving.

Everyday acts of quiet giving

> "It is not how much we give but how much love we put into giving."—Mother Teresa

Giving does not always have to be grand or public. Neither is it just about responding to crises and emergencies. Giving can— and must—also be about the everyday acts of kindness that we perform for one another.

Take the story of a young girl who regularly visited an elderly woman in her neighbourhood. The woman had no family or friends nearby, and the girl would stop by her home every week to chat with her, read to her and help with small chores around the house. This meant the world to the woman, who felt seen, heard and cared for.

Sometimes, the most meaningful acts of giving are the quiet ones. Like the man who made it his daily routine to pick up litter on his way to work. He did not do it for recognition or praise, but simply because he believed in taking care of his environment and making a small contribution towards a cleaner and healthier world.

Small acts of giving may seem insignificant, but they have a profound impact on those around us. They are a reminder that we are all in this together, and that even the smallest gesture of kindness can make a difference. Like the smile we offer a stranger on the street, or the help we give to a colleague in need or the simple act of listening to a friend who is going through a tough time. Think about the last time you received a note of appreciation or a small gift from a friend or loved one. Maybe it was a cup of coffee or a bouquet of flowers. Maybe it was just a few kind words of encouragement. Or the last time someone held a door open for you, or let you go ahead of them in line. That small act of kindness probably made your day a little bit brighter.

Giving touches the soul and nourishes the spirit. When we give, we become part of something greater than ourselves, and we contribute to the betterment of the world.

Giving that binds communities

"We rise by lifting others."—Robert Ingersoll

Communities are built on a foundation of shared values, beliefs and traditions. These shared experiences create a sense of belonging that brings people together, forming the social bonds that hold us all in place. Giving is an essential part of this process, as it allows individuals to contribute to their community and to feel a sense of ownership and responsibility for its well-being.

For example, when a hurricane, earthquake or other catastrophic event strikes, people from all walks of life come together to provide aid to those affected. This outpouring of generosity and kindness creates a sense of solidarity and unity that can outlast the immediate crisis. This way, communities can demonstrate their care and concern for one another, and work towards a common goal of rebuilding and recovery.

Communities can be strengthened through philanthropy, which involves individuals or organizations giving to causes they believe in, be it healthcare, education or the environment. Community bonds can also be built through volunteerism, which involves giving time and effort towards a cause, without the expectation of receiving anything in return. Such efforts create a shared sense of purpose and accomplishment. Whether it be cleaning up a local park, serving meals at a homeless shelter or participating in a community event, the act of volunteering can bring people together in a meaningful way.

The sharing of skills and knowledge is another significant way to bring communities closer. For example, in many cities and towns, neighbours come together to create and nurture gardens, public parks and green spaces. By working together to beautify their surroundings, these neighbours can form deep bonds and build meaningful relationships.

Giving as part of culture and tradition

"No one has ever become poor by giving."—Anne Frank

The act of giving is a celebration of generosity and a reflection of the human spirit. In cultures around the world, giving is a deeply rooted tradition often accompanied by ceremony and ritual. From the lavish offerings of ancient civilizations to the humble gifts exchanged between friends, the act of giving brings out humanity's most noble impulses.

In the East, the tradition of giving is woven into the fabric of everyday life. In Japan, the art of gift-giving is called *omiyage*. It is the cherished and revered act of bringing back souvenirs from one's travels to share with family, friends and colleagues. The Japanese believe that the act of giving gifts should be thoughtful and personal, reflecting the giver's gratitude and respect for the recipient. Omiyage is often beautifully wrapped in delicate paper, tied with ribbon and adorned with intricate decorations. The presentation of the gift is as important as the gift itself, and the giver takes great care in the way they wrap and present it.

In China too, the act of giving is steeped in tradition and symbolism. Red envelopes, known as *hong bao*, are given on special occasions such as Chinese New Year, weddings and birthdays. The envelopes are often adorned with gold or silver decorations and are filled with money or gifts. The colour red is considered auspicious in Chinese culture, symbolizing luck and prosperity.

In India, charity is known as *daan* and it is seen as a way to purify the soul and create good karma. It is an expression of love and devotion and is considered a sacred act. In Hindu society, gifts are often given to the gods and goddesses as offerings, and to priests as a sign of respect. It is customary to give gifts during festivals, weddings and other significant events. Gifts can range from simple items such as flowers and sweets to more elaborate offerings such as saris and precious jewellery.

In many African cultures, gift-giving is a way of strengthening social ties and showing respect for elders. The act of giving is known as *ubuntu* and is a way of demonstrating a person's interconnectedness with others. It is common to bring gifts of food such as fresh fruit or homemade bread when visiting someone's home. The Masai tribe in Kenya, for example, exchange intricately beaded necklaces, which are worn as a symbol of honour and prestige. The exchange of these necklaces is done in a ritualistic manner with much fanfare and celebration. The Masai also have a tradition called *emanyatta*, where young men come together to build a communal house for the newlyweds in the village. This act of giving is a symbol of the community's support for the new couple, and it is also an opportunity for the young men to showcase their skills and strength.

In Native American cultures, gift-giving is often associated with spiritual practices and healing. The act of giving a gift is seen as a way to express gratitude to the earth and its natural resources, and to honour the connection between all living beings. In some tribes, a healer may give a gift to a patient as a way of expressing gratitude for the opportunity to help heal them.

In the Middle East, gift-giving is often accompanied by a ceremony known as *mabrook*, which is performed to mark a significant achievement by someone, such as a new job or the birth of a child. Guests bring gifts, such as gold jewellery or cash, and the occasion is celebrated with food and music.

In many Western cultures, gift-giving is often associated with Christmas and other holidays. The tradition of giving gifts during these holidays has its roots in the story of the Three Wise Men, who brought gifts of gold, frankincense and myrrh to the newborn Jesus. Today, gift-giving during the holidays is a way of expressing love and appreciation for family and friends.

The 8-H Principle: A guide to achieving a fulfilled life

How do you make the journey of life fulfilling? I believe that the answer lies in the 8-H Principle, which is based on eight core values:
1. Honesty
2. Hard work,
3. Hobby,
4. Holiday,
6. Health,
7. Humility
7. Humanity and
8. Hope.

These are a set of guiding principles that can help individuals lead a purposeful life. In this book, we will look at each of these values in depth.

Hard work performed with dedication and perseverance is essential for success and cultivates a strong work ethic. Honesty fosters transparency and trust in personal and professional relationships, grounding one in authenticity and integrity. Humility opens doors to growth by acknowledging one's limitations. Hobbies provide vital self-care and relaxation, contributing to a balanced life, while holidays are crucial for rest and rejuvenation, and reducing stress and nurturing creativity. Prioritizing health—encompassing physical, mental and emotional well-being—enhances the overall quality of life. Humanity, characterized by compassion and kindness, nurtures strong relationships and ultimately benefits society. Lastly, hope, a powerful motivator, empowers us to overcome challenges and maintain optimism in pursuit of our goals. These elements collectively create a framework for a purpose-driven, fulfilling life.

Thus, the 8-H Principle helps us focus on key areas that emphasize perseverance, compassion, self-care and creativity, thereby promoting a comprehensive approach to life. It is my belief that by incorporating these eight values in our daily lives, we can build strong relationships, achieve success, fulfil our lives and make a positive impact on the world around us.

1 HONESTY

> *"Honesty is not a tool for your personal gain or your personal convenience. It is the foundation upon which your entire life is built."* —Oprah Winfrey

Shobha worked for a big corporation. She had worked tirelessly for years to make her way up the ladder, and was known not only for her perseverance and dedication, but also for her unwavering honesty.

One day, Shobha was tasked with working on a major project. Soon, she realized that there were some serious flaws in it that could harm the company and its clients. Knowing full well that she had to speak up, Shobha carefully drafted a report outlining her concerns. Her boss was initially dismissive of the report and told Shobha she was overthinking. But Shobha refused to back down, insisting that her concerns were valid and that the company needed to act.

Her boss eventually relented and agreed to hold a meeting with all the teams to address Shobha's concerns. The meeting was tense; many pushed back against Shobha's ideas, but she calmly and confidently presented her evidence and argued her case. In the end, the company took her concerns seriously and reworked the project to address the flaws, thereby saving millions and avoiding a public relations disaster. Shobha's bravery and honesty had paid off.

But Shobha's victory came at a cost. At first, many of her colleagues disliked her for "causing trouble"; they ostracized her and at times even threatened her. But over time, they began to see the wisdom in her actions. They came to respect her, and many even apologized for their earlier behaviour. Shobha had won not only the battle, but also the hearts of her colleagues. Her story became a legend within the company. Her conviction had saved the day, and her colleagues had learned a valuable lesson about the power of honesty. Shobha had triumphed, not just for herself but for the greater good.

Honesty is not a choice, but a must

Today, honesty such as Shobha's is rare. Lies, misinformation and half-truths have become the norm rather than the exception, and we are constantly bombarded with false promises and deceitful practices, be it by politicians or businesses.

The internet is a powerful tool for sharing knowledge, but it has also led to an increase in fake news, misinformation and propaganda. With so much available at our fingertips, it is easy to get misled and make decisions based on false information. This is why honesty has become crucial: we need to be able to trust the sources of information we rely on and ensure that information is accurate.

Honesty is often considered a virtue and a fundamental aspect of human integrity. Many argue that it is not merely a choice, but rather an underlying value that shapes our character and our relationships with others. Honesty involves more than just telling the truth; it implies being transparent, authentic and genuine in our interactions. It requires a commitment to ethical behaviour and a willingness to take responsibility for our actions and words. Conversely, when we choose to be dishonest, we risk eroding trust and damaging relationships.

Our world has become increasingly complex in the face of challenges such as climate change, economic inequality and social injustice. This requires us to work together to find solutions. To do this effectively, we need to be able to trust each other and work towards a common goal. Honesty is a key ingredient in this essential enterprise, and that is why honesty is not a choice anymore—it is a must.

Honesty as a business strategy

In the business world, honesty has become increasingly important owing to the advent of social responsibility and sustainability. Consumers are more aware than ever of the impact of their choices on the environment and on society, and are demanding more transparency and honesty from businesses. Companies that prioritize honesty and ethical practices are more likely to attract and retain customers, thereby succeeding in the long run.

Once there was a small business owner named Sarah who ran a bakery popular for its delicious cakes, pastries and pies, which she made using high-quality ingredients and traditional methods. No wonder she had many loyal customers. Then one day, Sarah noticed that her sales were declining. She simply could not figure out the problem, as she had neither changed the quality of her products nor made her prices less competitive. So, she decided to conduct a survey of her customers.

The survey revealed that many of her customers thought her products were still great, but they were no longer relevant to their needs. They were looking for healthier options, such as gluten-free, low-fat and low-sugar alternatives. Sarah realized she needed to adapt to these changing needs. Instead of compromising on the quality of her products or misleading her customers, she decided to be honest about the changes she was making. She introduced a new line of products that catered to her customers' dietary requirements, and she made sure to clearly label them. She shared her journey on social media and her website, explaining why she was making these changes and how it was important to stay relevant in today's world. Thanks to her honesty and willingness to adapt, Sarah's business began to thrive once again.

The multifaceted nature of honesty

> "Honesty is more than not lying. It is truth telling, truth speaking, truth living, and truth loving."—James E. Faust

In common parlance, an honest person is one who speaks the truth. However, the meaning of honesty goes beyond such a simple definition. In fact, honesty is a multifaceted concept that involves not only telling the truth, but also being transparent, authentic and vulnerable.

Being transparent means being open about our thoughts, feelings and actions. It involves sharing information willingly and without hesitation. When we are transparent, we show that we have nothing to hide and that we are willing to be held accountable for our actions.

Authenticity means being true to ourselves and our values, and being genuine in our interactions with others. When we are authentic, we are more likely to be perceived as trustworthy and reliable, which can lead to stronger relationships in both our personal and professional lives.

We might not always think about it, but vulnerability is also a critical component of honesty. Being vulnerable means taking risks and putting ourselves in situations in which we can get hurt or rejected. Vulnerability can be challenging, but it is essential in building deep and meaningful relationships. When we are vulnerable, we show that we trust others and are willing to let them see our true selves.

Honesty vs transparency

> "Honesty and transparency make you vulnerable. Be honest and transparent anyway."—Mother Teresa

Honesty and transparency are terms often used interchangeably. While both are related to the concept of truthfulness and openness, they are not the same thing. Understanding this difference is important.

Let us consider a workplace setting. An honest employee will tell the truth when asked a direct question, even if the answer may reflect poorly on them. A transparent employee, on the other hand, will not only answer the question truthfully but also provide additional information to help others understand the situation. For example, if an employee is asked if they made a mistake on a project, an honest response would be "Yes". A transparent response would be "Yes, I made a mistake, and here's what happened, this is how I plan to fix it and what I'll do differently in the future to prevent it from happening again".

Therefore, honesty and transparency are two equally important values. While honesty is about telling the truth, transparency is about showing the truth. Transparency is also associated with accountability, as it lets others hold us responsible for our actions. Both are essential for building strong relationships based on trust and mutual respect, and understanding the difference between the two can help us communicate more effectively in both our personal and professional lives.

Honesty as a virtue

Honesty has an evident moral and ethical dimension, and it is no surprise that all religions promote it as a fundamental value through various teachings, practices and traditions.

The Ten Commandments include "Thou shalt not bear false witness against thy neighbour." Prophet Muhammad is believed to have said, "Truthfulness leads to righteousness, and righteousness leads to Paradise." Buddhists believe that being truthful and honest is essential to developing wisdom and compassion, and lying and deception create negative karma, leading to suffering.

Chapter 17, Verse 15 of the Bhagavad Gita states that actions performed without sincerity, honesty and faith are in the mode of darkness, which leads to ignorance and suffering. Furthermore, the text encourages individuals to be truthful even in difficult situations. Chapter 16, Verse 2 states that one who speaks the truth and does what is right is freed from fear, anger and all forms of distress. And in Chapter 18, Verse 46, emphasis is laid on honesty in carrying out one's obligations: "By performing one's natural occupation, one worships the Creator from whom all living entities have come into being, and by whom the whole universe is pervaded. By such performance of work, a person easily attains perfection."

The art of honesty

>"Honesty without tact is just cruelty with a halo."
>—Bryant H. McGill

But simply being honest may not always be enough. In fact, when discussing sensitive matters, being blunt with our words can cause more harm than good. That is why it is essential to learn the art of honesty, that is, to approach difficult conversations with thoughtfulness and respect. By doing so, we can be both truthful and mindful of others' feelings.

Let me share a story. A young woman named Yasmin had always prided herself on being honest, even if it meant saying things that others might not want to hear. She believed that being straightforward was the best way to build strong relationships and earn the respect of others. Her new boss Mitali seemed friendly enough initially. But as Yasmin began to work on projects for the agency's clients, she realized that Mitali had a tendency to overpromise and underdeliver. Yasmin knew that this could hurt the agency's reputation and cost it clients in the long run.

One day, during a team meeting, Mitali presented a new campaign that Yasmin knew was destined to fail. True to her character, Yasmin spoke up, saying that the campaign would not work. Mitali was taken aback by this bluntness and became defensive. In the days that followed, Yasmin could feel the tension growing between her and Mitali, and she began to worry that she had made a mistake.

A few weeks later, Yasmin was called into Mitali's office and informed that her contract was being terminated. Mitali told her that she appreciated her honesty but that the agency needed someone who was more willing to go along with the company's plans, even if they were not perfect. Yasmin was devastated. She had thought that her honesty would be an asset to the agency, but instead, it had cost her the job.

In the end, Yasmin learned an important lesson about the limits of being straightforward. While honesty is important, we must consider the timing and context of what we are saying. Sometimes, a little diplomacy can go a long way.

The art of honesty lies in finding a balance between truthfulness and compassion, which can help us navigate even the most challenging conversations with grace. Here are some points to keep in mind whenever we face a situation where we need to achieve the balance between being honest and not hurting someone's sentiments:

Use tactful communication

During disagreements or conflicts, emotions tend to run high. Take a step back and assess the situation before jumping into the conversation. We need to choose our words carefully to convey the truth in a sensitive and diplomatic way, and avoid being blunt or hurtful in our delivery.

Consider the necessity

Before sharing potentially hurtful information, we should ask ourselves: Is it genuinely necessary to disclose it? Or are we doing it to be spiteful and to please our own ego? Sometimes, it may be kinder to withhold certain details if they will not result in any meaningful benefit.

Consider the timing

Timing matters when sharing difficult truths. Find an appropriate moment when the other person is receptive and emotionally prepared to hear what we have to say, and when they are not especially vulnerable.

Be mindful of our tone and body language

We must pay attention to our tone of voice and body language, as they can significantly impact how our message gets conveyed to the person in front of us. We must try our best to maintain a calm and non-confrontational demeanour.

Use "I" statements

Expressing our thoughts and feelings using "I" statements helps take ownership of our perspective. For example, instead of saying, "You're wrong", we can say, "I see things differently". Or, instead of making accusatory statements like "You shouldn't have done this", rather say, "I felt hurt when . . ."

Avoid unnecessary detail

Share the necessary information but avoid overwhelming the person with too many details that may not be relevant or helpful.

Offer constructive feedback

One of the awkward moments that we often face, especially in the workplace, is when we have to provide criticism or feedback. In such situations, we need to focus on sharing suggestions for improvement rather than just pointing out flaws.

Offer support

If we have to break a difficult news to someone, let the person know that we are there to support them and that we care about their well-being.

Listen actively

After we have shared the truth, we must actively listen to the other person's response and be open to their feelings and reactions. Their emotions are valid, and it is important that we acknowledge them.

Maintain confidentiality

If someone confides in us with sensitive information, we must respect their trust and keep the information confidential—unless, of course, there are ethical or legal reasons not to do so. This builds trust and strengthens relationships even when there is conflict or disagreement.

Remember that honesty is about integrity and transparency, but it should also be tempered with kindness and consideration for the feelings of others. Strive to balance truthfulness with empathy. Our goal should be to convey the truth in a way that preserves the other person's dignity and emotional health.

How to cultivate self-honesty

> "No need to hurry. No need to sparkle. No need to be anybody but oneself."—Virginia Woolf

We tend to value honesty in our interactions with others, but its importance in our relationship with ourselves is often overlooked. Let us call it self-honesty—an attribute that requires a willingness to face our own truths, even when they are painful. It implies being vulnerable and confronting aspects of ourselves that we do not like or are wary to change. It might seem challenging, but without self-honesty, there can be no true personal growth or meaningful interpersonal relationships.

When we are not honest with ourselves, we create a division between who we are and who we want to be. We deceive ourselves into believing that we are happy with our lives, our relationships or our careers—when in reality, we are not. This can make us feel disconnected from ourselves, and eventually dissatisfied, confused and even depressed.

On the other hand, in practising self-honesty, we become more self-aware, gaining a deeper understanding of our strengths and weaknesses, our values and beliefs, and our goals and aspirations. This self-awareness allows us to make more informed decisions, set realistic goals, and pursue our passions with greater clarity and purpose.

Self-honesty also enables us to take responsibility for our actions and their consequences. Instead of blaming others or external circumstances, we can acknowledge our role in creating our problems and take steps to address them. This empowers us to make positive changes in our lives and to become more resilient in the face of challenges.

As the philosopher Søren Kierkegaard once said in his book *The Sickness Unto Death*, "The greatest hazard of all, losing one's self, can occur very quietly in the world, as if it were nothing at all. No other loss can occur so quietly; any other loss—an arm, a leg, five dollars, a wife, etc.—is sure to be noticed."

Therefore, it is critical that we prioritize self-honesty in our lives to avoid losing ourselves in the pursuit of external validation or societal expectations.

But how do we cultivate self-honesty? I have some concrete tips to share:

Observe ourselves

It is important to simply observe our behaviour without trying to change anything. Approach this in a non-judgemental manner and we will recognize when we are not being honest with ourselves.

Practise journaling

Writing down our thoughts, feelings and experiences can help us process them more objectively. We can also identify patterns of behaviour or thought that may be hindering our progress.

Ask ourselves tough questions

Am I the person I want to be? What is my purpose in life? What regrets might I have on my deathbed? What would I do differently if I had no constraints or limitations? Asking ourselves difficult questions such as these will help us gain a deeper understanding of our motivations, fears and desires. It is important to not shy away from uncomfortable truths.

Challenge our beliefs

Are our beliefs and values truly our own or simply inherited from society or our family? We need to ask ourselves this and be open-minded and willing to change our beliefs if they no longer serve us.

Seek feedback

It is important to ask for honest feedback from people we trust. We will gain a more accurate perspective on ourselves. We must be open to constructive criticism and use it as an opportunity for growth.

It is crucial to remember that self-honesty is a continuous practice that requires introspection, and it may take time to develop this skill. We must be patient with ourselves and approach the process with curiosity and a willingness to learn.

Types of lies

No exploration of honesty can be complete without dwelling on dishonesty, which comes in different sizes and colours.

The reasons behind small, white lies

> "A white lie is like a snowball; the longer you roll it, the bigger it becomes."—Martin Luther King Jr.

I am sure we have all told a friend that we like their new hairstyle when we actually don't. Or told someone that we are busy when we just want to be alone. We tell these "white lies" or minor falsehoods in order to spare someone's feelings or avoid conflicts, in situations where telling the truth would be hurtful, awkward or inappropriate. White lies are social lubricants that help people navigate complex situations without causing unnecessary tension. One might say that white lies are part and parcel of the "art of honesty" as we have discussed earlier. But it is not always so. We will get into that in a little bit. But first, let us understand why we resort to white lies.

To avoid conflict

We often fear that telling the truth may lead to an argument or hurt someone's feelings, so we opt for a less truthful response, which is at the same time less confrontational.

To maintain social harmony

White lies can help maintain social harmony and smooth interactions. If we tell our colleague that their new flowery shirt looks great, even if we think it is neither stylish nor appropriate for office wear, it will most likely prevent tension or awkwardness in our conversation with him.

To preserve self-esteem

Our instinct for the preservation of self-esteem is one of the most serious reasons why we tell white lies. This includes exaggerating our achievements or downplaying our mistakes to make ourselves look better in the eyes of others. For example, when asked about a recent job interview, someone might say, "They were really impressed with my skills and personality, but they decided to go with an internal candidate"—even though in reality, this person was not selected for the position at all. This white lie protected the person's self-esteem.

To avoid punishment or negative consequences

People may lie to avoid punishment or negative consequences, even when the stakes are relatively low. This can be especially common in children. Say eleven-year-old Aaryan forgot to do his homework because he was busy playing video games after school. The next morning when the teacher collects the homework assignments, Aaryan realizes he does not have it ready. Instead of telling the truth and getting a scolding or a lower grade, he says he had finished the homework but had left it at home by accident.

To alleviate guilt

Sometimes, we tell white lies to lessen our guilt. If we have made a mistake or let someone down, we may say things like, "I did all I could" or "I tried my best" even if we did not make a sincere effort. On a lighter note, perhaps, we might tell our friend, "I couldn't make it to your party last night because I was not feeling well". In truth, we skipped the party to relax at home, but we tell this white lie to alleviate our guilt for not attending.

To maintain privacy

White lies can be used to protect our privacy or keep certain information confidential. For instance, if a co-worker asks if we are dating someone, we might choose to say no in order to keep our personal life confidential in a professional setting.

To safeguard relationships

White lies can be a way of protecting relationships by not burdening others with unnecessary or distressing information. Very often we may not disclose our own worries or concerns to avoid causing unnecessary worry to our loved ones. Take the example of Vasu, who is asked by a friend about Janet's recent break-up. Vasu says she has spoken to Janet and she has been keeping herself busy to focus on her self-care. In this example, Vasu tells a white lie by offering a simplified and more positive response to protect her friend Janet's privacy and avoid burdening the inquisitive friend with the potentially distressing details of Janet's recent break-up. Vasu is trying to maintain the relationship with her friend while respecting Janet's need for space during a difficult time.

As is evident from these examples, white lies are usually harmless. However, they can still be damaging. If we consistently tell our friend that we like their fashion choices when we actually don't, they may continue to dress in a way that does not suit them, which could harm their social standing as well as their self-esteem. Always consider the impact of the lie on the person to whom it is being told and weigh the potential consequences of telling the truth versus telling a lie.

Telling white lies can become a part of a person's character. When someone gets used to telling small lies to avoid discomfort or to protect their image, it gets easier to justify telling bigger lies to cope with complicated situations. As the lies become more significant, the fear of being exposed intensifies, and the person resorts to telling even bigger lies to cover up previous ones. This pattern of deception is hard to break, and the inevitable result is a breach of trust in valuable relationships.

Take the story of Satish. His lies started small but grew bigger over time. He lied about his accomplishments, his financial status and even his relationships, for he believed lying was the best way to impress people. However, people eventually caught on to his lies and started to distance themselves from him. One day, Satish's lies caught up with him when he told his boss that he had completed a project when in reality he had not. When his boss found out, he fired Satish, who then realized that what began as a habit of telling white lies had gone out of control. Satish and his existence had become inextricably linked to one lie after another. And this had caused him to lose so much: his job, his standing in society and even, eventually, his marriage. He decided to change his ways and start telling the truth. Slowly, with the right attitude, he was able to begin rebuilding his life.

If we find ourselves frequently resorting to telling white lies, it will be useful to examine the underlying psychological reasons for this pattern—the points we have discussed above. It is essential to recognize when a habit of lying is becoming problematic and address it before it spirals out of control. The best thing would be to seek help from a therapist to understand the root causes of the behaviour and develop healthy coping mechanisms. But I can share a few tips about where we might want to start:

Reflect and keep a journal: We need to examine why we lie chronically. Is it to avoid conflict, gain approval, or protect ourselves? Understanding the root causes of our lying behaviour is essential. Keep a journal to track our lies and the situations that trigger them. This self-awareness can help us identify patterns and triggers.

Take accountability and apologize: We must take responsibility for our past lies and their consequences. Apologize to those we have lied to and make amends wherever possible. Acknowledging our actions and their impact is an important step in rebuilding trust of others—and it relieves us of huge emotional and mental pressure.

Set realistic expectations: We must understand and acknowledge that nobody is perfect. Occasional lapses in honesty are bound to happen in everyone's life. Instead of being discouraged by these lapses, we must use them as opportunities for self-reflection and growth. There is no alternative to learning from our experiences, even if they are mistakes.

Surround ourselves with supportive people: We must seek out friends and family members who can understand and encourage us as we work to overcome the habit of lying. Having a supportive network makes the process much less daunting.

Practise honesty gradually: We must commit to telling the truth, even if it is uncomfortable or difficult. We could start with small, low-stakes situations and slowly work our way up to major challenges. It is important to understand that it may take a while for people to believe that we have changed, and they may still be cautious. Building a habit of honesty takes time and practice. But it is still worth it.

Big, black lies

The "big lie" or the "black lie" is a tactic that has been used throughout history to manipulate and control people by disseminating false information. The term "big lie" was coined by Adolf Hitler in his infamous book *Mein Kampf* (1925). He believed that if a lie was repeated often enough, people would eventually accept it as truth—a falsehood so outrageous that no one would think it could have been invented. Hitler used this tactic to convince the Germans that the Jews were responsible for Germany's problems and that they needed to be eliminated. This big lie ultimately led to the Holocaust.

The big lie is a powerful propaganda technique that preys on people's fears and prejudices. It provides a simple explanation for complex problems and creates a sense of unity among those who believe it. The most dangerous thing about a big lie is that it is often difficult to distinguish it from the truth—because it is mixed with some modicum of truth, making it appear plausible. By being repeated by those in positions of authority and influence, the big lie gains credibility. The consequences of the big lie can be devastating, leading to the demonization of entire groups of people, discrimination, violence and even genocide. It also creates a climate of distrust and division in society.

It is essential to protect ourselves from the power of the big lie. But how?

How to protect ourselves from big, black lies

Here are a few ways:

Diversify our information sources

It is best not to depend on one news channel or newspaper for our news, but rely on a variety of reputable sources for information on current and past events. Avoid "echo chambers" where we only hear one perspective. Diversifying our sources can provide a more balanced view of current events and reduce the risk of falling victim to big lies.

Check the credibility of sources

Before trusting a source, we must assess its credibility—consider the reputation of the media outlet, the author and the publication date. Fact-checking organizations can help us verify the accuracy of information.

Develop critical thinking and media literacy

This involves being sceptical of claims that seem too good to be true or too outrageous. We must fact-check information before accepting it as truth, and be aware of confirmation bias.

Learn about disinformation tactics

We must familiarize ourselves with common disinformation tactics, such as clickbait headlines, deepfakes, selective editing, and manipulated images and videos. Understanding these tactics can make us more discerning when faced with content that may be deceptive or false.

Be mindful of emotional responses

As discussed earlier, big lies mainly target emotive issues to provoke strong reactions. We should be aware of our emotional responses to information, and take a step back to carefully and critically evaluate the information before reacting or sharing it on social media.

Teach media literacy to others

We can do a lot by sharing our knowledge of media literacy and critical thinking with family and friends. Encourage them to question the information they encounter online and offline. Collective efforts to combat misinformation and big lies can have a significant impact.

We must not forget that like everything else, dealing with big lies is an ongoing process. The media scenario is always shifting and evolving, and staying vigilant and informed is key to protecting ourselves from the harmful effects of big lies and rampant misinformation in this digital age.

Raising honest kids: Lessons for parents

> "Teaching children to be honest with themselves and others is one of the most important things we can do as parents."—Brené Brown

In the end, is it enough to be just honest ourselves? Shouldn't honesty be a legacy, something we can propagate for the betterment of all? As parents, do we not all want our children to grow up to be responsible, honest and successful individuals? One way to help them achieve these is by instilling in them the value of honesty. If we teach children the value of honesty, it can help them build strong and healthy relationships throughout their lives. Here are some techniques to adopt:

Model honesty

Children learn from what they see and hear, so it is essential to model honesty in our actions and words. We should be truthful with our children, admit to our mistakes and show them how to take responsibility for their actions.

Teach the importance of honesty

We should explain to our children the importance of honesty in building trust, relationships and personal integrity, and also provide them with examples of how honesty has helped us in our lives.

Lead by example

There is no option but to lead by example. This means pursuing our passions, giving back to our communities and making a positive impact on the world around us. Children will learn from what they see in us.

Encourage truth-telling

We must praise our children when they tell the truth, even if it means admitting to something they did wrong. This will reinforce the importance of honesty and encourage them to continue to be truthful.

Set clear expectations

It is important to let our child know that honesty is always the best policy and that there will be consequences if they lie or deceive others.

Teach problem-solving skills

We help our children learn how to handle difficult situations by encouraging them to come up with creative solutions based on honesty and integrity.

Reinforce honesty through tales

We can use stories and games to help our child learn about honesty in a fun and engaging way.

Be patient

Remember that learning to be honest is a process, and it may take time for our children to fully understand its gravity. We must be patient and understanding, and continue to reinforce the importance of honesty in their lives.

Conclusion

Honesty is a fundamental and universal value that all individuals should aspire to embody—which is why it is the bedrock of the 8-H Principle. Beyond being a moral imperative, honesty is a practical necessity for success in life. Honesty serves as the foundation upon which trust is constructed, underpinning both personal and professional relationships. When people perceive us as honest, they tend to place their trust in us, nurturing strong, meaningful connections.

Secondly, honesty fosters an environment for open communication, allowing individuals to comfortably express their thoughts and emotions. This, in turn, cultivates understanding, mutual respect and cooperation. Moreover, honesty lessens the chances of conflict and misunderstanding by promoting transparency. Such transparency always contributes to harmonious and peaceful relationships.

At a more personal level, honesty leads to self-awareness through truthful appraisal of one's strengths and weaknesses. This is essential for positive personal growth.

Lastly, honesty contributes to building a positive reputation in society. It earns respect and admiration when coupled with integrity, making it an indispensable quality for a good public image. Hence, honesty emerges as an indispensable value crucial to our everyday lives bringing together trust, communication, integrity, conflict resolution, self-awareness, respect and reputation.

2 HARD WORK

> "There is no elevator to success, you have to take the stairs." —Zig Ziglar

It is a truth universally acknowledged that hard work is the foundation of success. Let me begin with a story of one incredible individual who has achieved a great deal in life—Jack Ma, the co-founder and former executive chairman of Alibaba Group, one of the world's largest e-commerce companies. Born in 1964 in Hangzhou, China, Jack Ma grew up poor and faced numerous rejections in his early life. He struggled in school and was even rejected from jobs at KFC and the police force. But he persevered and taught himself English by practising speaking with foreign tourists in Hangzhou.

In the mid-1990s, Jack Ma saw the huge potential for e-commerce and founded Alibaba in 1999 with a group of friends. The company started as a business-to-business e-commerce platform, connecting Chinese manufacturers with buyers around the world. In spite of facing numerous challenges, including the dot-com bubble burst and competition from other e-commerce giants, Jack Ma and his team continued to work tirelessly to grow Alibaba into the behemoth it is today. Under his leadership, Alibaba went public in 2014, raising a record-breaking $25 billion in its initial public offering.

Today, Jack Ma is one of the richest people in China, with a net worth of nearly $50 billion. He has become a philanthropist and is known for his work for education and environmental causes. Despite his success, he remains humble and continues to inspire others with his story of hard work and determination. Hard work is the key to achieving our goals and the hallmark of a strong, resilient character. Whether we are striving for personal growth, career advancement or simply a better life, hard work is essential to our success. In this chapter, I will explore the significance of hard work and discuss how it can help us achieve our dreams.

The necessity of hard work

Hard work is critical for achieving success in any aspect of life. While talent and intelligence are important, they alone cannot guarantee success. It is the diligence, persistence and effort that we put in our goals that determines their level of achievement. Hard work is necessary to turn talent and intelligence into something tangible and worthwhile. Before delving into details, let us summarize why hard work is essential in our lives:

Achieving goals

Hard work is essential to achieve success. When we work hard towards our goals, we develop the necessary skills, knowledge and experience to succeed.

Personal growth

When we work hard, we learn new skills, gain knowledge and develop the ability to overcome challenges. This can help us grow as a person and become more resilient, confident and capable.

Satisfaction and fulfilment

Working hard towards something we value and achieving it gives us a sense of pride and accomplishment, which can be very satisfying.

Opportunities

When we work hard and produce results, we are more likely to be recognized and given new opportunities to advance our career.

Discipline and focus

When we work hard, we learn to prioritize our time, stay focused on our goals and avoid distractions. These skills can help us in many areas of our life.

Mastery

By putting in the time and effort to practice, study and learn, we can become highly proficient in a particular area.

Persistence

It is inevitable that we will face obstacles, setbacks and failures along the way to success. But if we are willing to put in the effort and keep pushing forward, we will be better equipped to overcome these challenges. Through hard work, we learn the value of persistence.

Productivity

When we commit ourselves to working hard, we are more likely to use our time efficiently, be productive and get more done in less time.

The spiritual foundation of hard work

Hard work is not just a tool to further our career. There is a deep spiritual dimension to it as well. This is why many religions around the world extol its virtues. For believers, working hard and doing so with honesty and integrity can be a way to connect with the divine, to honour and express gratitude for the gifts of life and to fulfil a higher purpose.

Hard work and honest labour are seen by some as a way to cultivate discipline, focus and self-improvement. For example, in Buddhism, the concept of "right livelihood" emphasizes the importance of earning a living in a way that is ethical and beneficial to others. This means avoiding work that causes harm, such as dealing in weapons, drugs or exploiting others, and instead focusing on activities that promote well-being, such as teaching, healing or creating. Through this practice, Buddhists believe they can cultivate a sense of purpose and meaning in their work as well as reduce suffering in the world.

The Quran teaches that hard work and perseverance are necessary for success in this life and the next. The Hadith states, "No one has ever eaten better food than that which one has earned by one's own hands" (Sahih al-Bukhari 2072). Furthermore, the idea of "halal" work emphasizes the importance of earning a living in a lawful, honest and dignified way. This work ethic is seen as a way to honour God's blessings and to contribute to the welfare of society, while also achieving personal growth and fulfilment.

In the Bible, the apostle Paul writes, "Whatever you do, work heartily, as for the Lord and not for men" (Colossians 3:23 ESV). This verse emphasizes the idea that hard work is not only for earthly rewards, but also a way to honour and demonstrate faith and gratitude for God's gifts. Jesus was known as a hard-working carpenter, and his parables often emphasized the importance of diligent and responsible labour.

Karma Yoga teaches that when we do our duties with detachment, discipline and devotion, we can purify our mind and develop a deeper understanding of the divine nature of reality. Hard work is seen to transcend the ego and cultivate a sense of unity with the universe.

Therefore, the connection between hard work and religion goes beyond mere material success or personal achievement. It reflects a deeper spiritual insight into the nature of reality and our place in it.

The various forms of grit and perseverance

Hard work is often associated with long hours, sweat and perseverance. But that is reductive. In fact, hard work can take many different forms like:

Emotional labour

This refers to the effort required to manage and regulate one's own emotions as well as those of others. Emotional hard work involves being a good listener, providing emotional support and maintaining positive relationships. Examples include social work, counselling, caregiving and other jobs that require empathy and emotional intelligence. These are types of work that can be draining but deeply rewarding at the same time.

Intellectual labour

Many of us use our brainpower to solve complex problems, analyse data and develop innovative ideas. This is what intellectual labour is. It often requires extensive research, critical thinking and the ability to adapt to new situations. Intellectual work can be both challenging and exhilarating, and it often demands a great deal of focus and determination. Examples include critical writing, journalism, scientific research, etc.

Physical labour

Perhaps the quintessential image of hard work involves primarily using our body to perform tasks. Needless to say, physical work requires a lot of stamina and dedication to fitness, but it can also provide a sense of accomplishment and pride in our abilities. Examples include construction work, farming, manufacturing and other jobs that involve heavy lifting or manual labour.

Risk-taking labour

This type of hard work involves taking on challenges that require courage, determination and the willingness to face uncertainty and potential failure. Examples include starting a business, pursuing a risky career path or taking on a difficult project.

Creative labour

Using one's imagination and artistic abilities to produce something new and original is widely celebrated in our society, but this too involves a difficult form of labour. Be it creative writing, painting, composing music or any other form of art which requires a great deal of inspiration and dedication.

Each type of hard work demands a unique set of skills and qualities. But whether it is emotional, intellectual or physical labour, hard work is a vital ingredient for success in all aspects of life.

How to achieve smart, strategic and result-oriented hard work

There is an old saying, "Hard work beats talent when talent doesn't work hard." While intelligence and talent can certainly give one an initial advantage, without hard work that advantage quickly dissipates. On the other hand, a person who is willing to put in the time and effort to learn and improve often surpasses those who rely solely on their natural abilities. This is because hard work not only allows us to develop skills and knowledge, but also fosters discipline, focus and determination. These qualities are crucial for success in any field or endeavour.

Now, we can work very hard, but without a clear plan or strategy we will not find the success we crave. All we will have to show at the end are inefficient use of resources and wasted effort. So, it is imperative that we focus on smart, strategic and result-oriented work. Here are some tips as to how to go about it:

Prioritize our tasks

It is essential to make a to-do list of our tasks and prioritize them based on their importance and urgency. To-do lists can be (i) daily, (ii) weekly (iii) monthly and so on. Focus on the most urgent tasks first and try to delegate or eliminate tasks that are not essential.

Break tasks into smaller parts

It is no surprise that large tasks can seem overwhelming, so we could try breaking them down into smaller parts. Making incremental progress on our work will help us stay determined. Every time we tick off a small task from our list, we will feel motivated by our accomplishment.

Take breaks

Taking short breaks can help us recharge and stay focused. We can try taking a five-minute break every hour or so, or take a longer break after completing a major task.

Use technology to our advantage

There are numerous tools and applications at our disposal that can enhance our productivity, for example, time-tracking apps, project management software and automation tools. Emerging artificial intelligence solutions like ChatGPT and Bard offer novel opportunities to leverage technology to our advantage, enabling us to significantly save time and facilitating faster, more efficient work.

Avoid multitasking

Multitasking is a hallowed word in many circles. When we are able to juggle several tasks at the same time, we are considered to be a paragon of leadership and efficiency. But the truth is that multitasking leads to distractions, compromising focus and hence decreasing productivity. Instead of multitasking, we should try to focus on one task at a time and complete it before moving on to the next.

Learn to say no

I cannot overemphasize the value of this mantra. It can be tempting to agree to do many tasks, believing that the more we take on, the better we are as a worker. But if we learn to say no, we can focus on our most important priorities and avoid burnout from overwork.

Invest in our skills

Learning new skills or improving the existing ones will help us work more efficiently and effectively. It is important that we take courses, attend conferences or read books—such as this one—to develop our skills and knowledge.

Practise good time management

We should set realistic deadlines for our tasks and try to stick to them. While the temptation to push ourselves to complete tasks in record time may boost our self-esteem, such a tendency often leads to overwork. And what is more, it results in hastily finished, incomplete, error-prone or subpar work. Instead of rushing through projects or tasks, we must take the time to realistically assess how long they should take to be done properly. And accordingly, set ourselves achievable timeframes and goals.

This kind of focused and effective hard work is highly relevant in today's world, where competition is fierce, and success is highly valued. It allows individuals to develop skills, knowledge, discipline and resilience, at the same time fostering a sense of personal accountability. Ultimately, focused work can inspire and motivate others to work harder, perform better and strive for their success.

A guide to effectively tackling the to-do list

As our lives get increasingly busier, it has become more important than ever to prioritize our tasks to make the most of our time. But when we have a long list of to-dos, it can be overwhelming to decide where to start. No two persons can work in the exact same way. So to get everything done efficiently, it is crucial to develop a prioritization system that works for us. Here are a few tips that can help:

Identify urgent vs important tasks

It is important to determine which tasks are urgent (need to be completed immediately) and which ones are important (have a long-term impact). Urgent tasks should be given priority, but important tasks should not be neglected either.

Set goals and deadlines

When we establish clear goals and deadlines for each task, it helps us stay on track and focus on the tasks that need to be completed first.

Evaluate the potential impact

We need to consider the impact each task can have. Some tasks may have a greater influence on our work or organization, so it is important to prioritize those.

Consider the relations between tasks

Consider tasks that depend on others. If completing one task is necessary for another, we should prioritize the one that needs to be done first.

Keep in mind our strengths

Identify the tasks that play to our strengths and complete those first. This can help us build momentum and motivation to tackle more challenging tasks later.

Use a prioritization matrix

A prioritization matrix can help us determine which tasks to focus on first based on their level of importance and urgency. This can be a useful tool for decision-making. Prioritization is a continuous process, so we must regularly review and adjust our priorities as needed to stay on track and achieve our goals.

Ultimately, the key to mastering prioritization is to develop a system that we find suitable and follow it consistently. With a little practice and discipline, we can learn to manage our to-do list like a pro and achieve our goals with ease.

The importance of consistency

In 2009, Susan Boyle became an overnight sensation after appearing on the UK reality show *Britain's Got Talent*. Born in 1961 in Blackburn, Scotland, she had always dreamed of becoming a professional singer. Despite her passion for music and her talent, Susan had struggled to make a career in the industry and had never performed in front of a large audience. When she walked onto the stage of *Britain's Got Talent* and announced that she wanted to sing "I Dreamed a Dream" from the musical *Les Misérables*, the judges and the audience were sceptical. But as soon as she began to sing, the room fell silent and everyone was captivated by her stunning voice.

The video of Susan's performance went viral, and within days, she became an international sensation. Her first album, *I Dreamed a Dream*, became UK's bestselling debut album ever. She appeared on countless talk shows, was interviewed by major news outlets and was even invited to perform at the opening ceremony of the 2014 Commonwealth Games in front of the Queen of England.

However, despite her initial success, Susan Boyle struggled to maintain consistency in her career. Her subsequent albums and performances failed to match the success of her debut. She took part in *America's Got Talent* in 2019 but failed to win the competition.

Susan's story serves as a powerful reminder of the importance of consistency in achieving long-term success. While a one-time spark can provide a powerful boost to a career or project, it is only through sustained effort and dedication that true success can be achieved.

Consistency is the ability to maintain a regular and predictable pattern of behaviour or performance, even in the face of challenges or obstacles. Consistency is especially important in fields where public attention and recognition play a significant role, such as entertainment, sports and social media. In these arenas, individuals who achieve a momentary spark of fame or popularity but fail to sustain it with consistent effort and improvement are often quickly forgotten.

The power of consistency

"Don't watch the clock; do what it does. Keep going."
—Sam Levenson

Consistency is a quality that sets apart successful people from those who struggle to reach their goals. Whether it is in our personal life, career or relationships, consistency is the foundation of success. Let us explore why consistency is so important, and how we can develop this crucial quality in our lives.

Builds habits

When we consistently act towards our goals, we create a habit of progress. We develop routines, making it easier for us to keep moving forward, even when we do not feel motivated or inspired.

Leads to mastery

When we consistently practise a skill or activity, we become better at it over time. Whether it is a sport, a musical instrument or a profession, consistency allows us to continually improve and develop our abilities.

Establishes trust

Consistently showing up on time, delivering on your promises and following through with your commitments lead to people trusting you. They know that they can rely on you to do what you say you will do, which builds credibility and strengthens your reputation.

Fosters discipline

Discipline is the ability to control our thoughts, emotions and actions, and to stay focused on our goals, even in the face of distractions and setbacks. Consistent action builds discipline, which is a crucial quality for achieving success.

Produces results

Consistency produces results, which is the ultimate goal of any endeavour. We make small gains every day, which add up over time and eventually lead to significant results.

Develops resilience

Consistency also helps develop resilience, which is the ability to bounce back from setbacks and keep moving forward.

Our struggle to stay focused

Despite knowing the importance of consistency, many of us struggle to stay on track. Let us see what the reasons are:

Distractions

Technology such as social media, email and text messages can be very distracting and take away from our ability to focus on a task. Furthermore, uncomfortable, noisy or cluttered work environments also affect our ability to work consistently. Unexpected interruptions such as phone calls or unexpected visitors often disrupt our workflow and lead to inconsistency.

Unexpected events

Life is full of surprises, and unexpected events can throw us off track and disrupt our routines. These include issues in our family, sudden health problems, and related stress and anxiety.

Negative self-talk

Any inner dialogue we have with ourselves that limits our ability to believe in ourselves and our own skills can sabotage our efforts and prevent us from taking consistent action. It is important to practise self-compassion and positive self-talk to stay motivated and focused.

Lack of accountability

Without a system of accountability, it can be easy to let our goals and intentions fall by the wayside. This also lets us slide into procrastination or delay tasks, leading to rushed and inconsistent work. Having an accountability partner or tracking our own progress helps maintain consistency.

Developing consistency requires commitment, dedication and a willingness to push through discomfort and challenges. The rewards are significant and the benefits of consistency extend far beyond achieving success. It is a quality that enhances our life and helps us become the best version of ourselves.

The challenges of consistent hard work

Very often, we dedicate ourselves to hard work and get lost in it. Working hard comes with its own set of challenges that can hinder progress if not addressed correctly and at the right time. Let us examine the biggest issues that individuals face when working hard and consistently performing well.

Burnout

Burnout is a state of emotional, physical and mental exhaustion that results from prolonged stress and overworking. It can manifest itself in several ways, including lack of motivation, decreased productivity, and increased feelings of cynicism and detachment. It is essential to recognize the early signs of burnout and take steps to prevent it, such as taking breaks, delegating tasks and seeking support.

Lack of work-life balance

Long hours and demanding schedules can lead to a lack of time for personal relationships, hobbies and self-care activities. It is crucial to prioritize self-care and take the time to engage in activities that promote overall well-being. Setting boundaries, scheduling time for relaxation and leisure activities, and practising mindfulness can all help achieve a better work-life balance.

Monotony

Repetitive tasks and a lack of variety in work can lead to monotony and decrease motivation and engagement. It is essential to find ways to make work more challenging and engaging, such as taking on new projects, learning new skills or seeking feedback and mentorship. Incorporating breaks and rewards for accomplishments can also help break up the monotony of consistent performance.

Perfectionism

A perfectionistic mindset can be both helpful and harmful. Perfectionism can drive individuals to achieve their goals and strive for excellence, but it can also lead to excessive self-criticism and fear of failure. It is essential to recognize the difference between healthy striving and harmful perfectionism and have compassion for oneself as well as be able to forgive oneself.

Imposter syndrome

Imposter syndrome is a feeling of inadequacy and self-doubt despite evidence of competence and success. Often high-performing individuals fall prey to this syndrome, which leads to decreased confidence, increased anxiety and poorer motivation. It is crucial to recognize this syndrome and seek support and validation from others.

Techniques for battling burnout

Burnout is a common issue that affects many people, especially those who work in high-stress environments. The signs are not hard to spot. Burnout can manifest through physical and emotional exhaustion, detachment from work and a reduced sense of accomplishment. It can be difficult to overcome burnout, but there are techniques that can help individuals manage their stress levels and keep burnout at bay. Let me summarize them here:

Prioritize self-care

I cannot emphasize enough the importance of taking care of ourselves in our efforts to prevent burnout. Self-care can include activities such as exercise, meditation, spending time with loved ones and engaging in hobbies or other leisure activities. By prioritizing self-care, we can better manage our stress levels and maintain consistent performance.

Practise time management

Individuals can become overwhelmed by their workload, leading to burnout. To prevent this, we should prioritize our tasks and create a schedule that allows us to balance our work and personal lives. This may involve delegating tasks to others, setting realistic deadlines and taking breaks throughout the day to recharge. Effective time management is critical to preventing burnout.

Set boundaries

We need to be aware of our limitations and communicate them to others. It is important to recognize that we cannot do everything, all at the same time. It is important to say no to additional tasks, set limits on work hours and take time off when needed. By setting boundaries, we can better manage our workload and prevent burnout.

Seek support

Support from others can provide us with the motivation and encouragement we need to overcome burnout and consistently perform our best. This may involve seeking guidance from a mentor or coach, speaking with a therapist or counsellor or simply confiding in a friend or family member.

The power of saying no

> "The difference between successful people and very successful people is that very successful people say no to almost everything."—Warren Buffett

In a world that values productivity and success, it is easy to keep saying yes to every opportunity that comes our way because we want to show that we are capable of taking on anything and everything. But the truth is that saying yes to everything is a trap that leads to stress, burnout and a lack of fulfilment.

We have all been there. The boss asks us to take on a new project, a friend asks for our help with something or a family member needs us to run an errand—in that moment, saying yes seems like the only option. But when we say yes too often, we risk overcommitting ourselves and taking on more than we can handle. We think that saying yes will lead to more opportunities and success. But when we say yes to everything, we spread ourselves thin and struggle to give our best effort to any one task. We become stressed, anxious and exhausted.

Saying no, on the other hand, allows us to prioritize our time and energy on the things that matter most. When we say no to something, we create space for something else. We give ourselves the opportunity to focus on our goals, our passions and our health and happiness.

Learning when to say yes and when to say no is an essential part of hard work, and it creates a reliable road to professional success as well as personal well-being. So let us explore ourselves a bit to understand this dilemma of saying yes or no, and to figure out how we can come out on top.

The psychology of saying yes

Why do we say yes to things too easily? Here are some reasons, which are important to understand if we are to get over this habit:

Desire to please others

People feel like they need to say yes to all requests to avoid disappointing or upsetting others. They may worry that saying no will make them seem uncooperative or difficult to work with.

Fear of conflict

Some people may be averse to conflict and feel uncomfortable saying no because they fear it may lead to tension in their relationships.

Lack of assertiveness

Some of us struggle with assertiveness and find it difficult to stand up for ourselves. We feel like we need to go along with what others want in order to avoid confrontation, and hence our easy answer is always yes.

Insecurity

Some individuals feel that saying no will make them appear less capable or valuable to others, leading them to say yes to everything.

Guilt or obligation

People may feel like they owe others something or have an obligation to help or support them, even if it comes at a personal cost.

Fear of missing out (FOMO)

Some of us worry that saying no to an opportunity or invitation will cause us to miss out on something important or fun.

Strategies for saying no without feeling guilty

> "When you say yes to others, make sure you are not saying no to yourself."—Paulo Coelho

To avoid falling into the "yes trap", it is important for us to be clear about our priorities, boundaries and needs. We should feel comfortable saying no when necessary and be confident in communicating our needs and preferences to others.

Here are some tips to escape the "yes trap":

Pause before responding

When someone asks you for a favour or to commit to something, take a moment to think before answering. This will give you time to consider your priorities and whether you have the time and resources to fulfil the request.

Ask for more information

Ask questions to clarify the details of the request, such as the timeline, the scope of work and the resources required. This will help you make an informed decision about whether you can commit to the request.

Do not overcommit

Be realistic about what you can accomplish and don't take on more than you can handle. If you are already overwhelmed with commitments, it is okay to decline new requests.

Prioritize your own goals

It is important to prioritize your own goals and values. If a request aligns with your own priorities and goals, you may be more likely to say yes, but if it does not align, it is okay to decline it.

Learn to say a polite no

Saying no can be difficult, but it is important to set boundaries and give priority to your own needs. You can decline politely by thanking the person for the opportunity but explaining that you are unable to commit at the time.

A guide to assertiveness and boundaries

Unsurprisingly, saying no can be easily viewed negatively. It can be seen as confrontational, or even rude, which makes it difficult for us to set personal boundaries and decline requests. This includes obligations conflicting with our priorities or values. However, saying no is crucial for self-care and for safeguarding time, energy and resources. It does not reflect weakness; rather, it shows self-respect and awareness. The honesty inherent in saying no actually enhances relationships through mutual respect and integrity.

Here are some tips for cultivating the art of saying no:

Identify our priorities and values

Knowing our priorities and values can help us determine which requests or obligations align with our goals and which do not. This can make it easier to say no to requests that do not serve our best interests.

Be respectful

Express gratitude for the opportunity or request, and acknowledge the other person's needs or feelings.

Provide a reason

Giving a reason for our refusal can help the other person understand our perspective and make it easier for them to accept our decision. However, we should not over-explain as that may appear as if we are feeling guilty about turning down an offer.

Use "I" statements

Instead of saying, "You can't expect me to do this", say, "I am unable to take on this task because it conflicts with my existing commitments."

Be clear

We need to state our decision clearly and succinctly, so that there is no scope for any misunderstanding.

Offer alternatives

If we are unable to say yes to a request, consider offering an alternative solution. For example, if a friend asks us out for dinner on a night when we have other plans, suggest another day or activity that works better for both of us.

Rejection as motivation

We have all heard the phrase "no means no" when it comes to setting boundaries and respecting others' decisions. We have just discussed how important it is in today's overworked world to say no. But being on the receiving end of "no" can be a disheartening experience. Yet, "no" can also be a powerful tool to prove a point.

We all face rejection at some point in our lives. Whether it is a job application, a romantic interest or even just a simple request, being told "no" can be disheartening. It can make us feel like we are not good enough or that our ideas are not worth pursuing.

But instead of letting rejection get the best of us, we can use it as fuel to ignite our passion and drive. For example, imagine you have pitched a new idea to your boss, and they shoot it down, saying it is not feasible. Instead of giving up, use their rejection as motivation to come up with a more compelling proposal.

One of the most remarkable stories of determination and hard work is that of Wilma Rudolph, who went on to become an Olympic champion despite being told "no" repeatedly in her life.

Wilma was born prematurely in 1940 in Clarksville, Tennessee. She was the twentieth of her father's twenty-two children and weighed only two kg at birth. She suffered from multiple health problems as a child, including scarlet fever, pneumonia and polio, which left her with a twisted left leg and foot. Doctors told her mother that Wilma would never walk and should be confined to a brace for the rest of her life.

However, Wilma's mother refused to accept this prognosis and took it upon herself to help her daughter learn to walk. She massaged Wilma's legs and feet several times a day and helped her practise walking with a brace. Wilma's determination paid off, and by the time she was twelve years old, she was able to walk without the brace.

Wilma's love of running began when she was in elementary school. She joined her school's basketball team and later ran in track and field competitions. Despite her physical challenges, Wilma was a gifted athlete and set records in many track events she entered. She not only qualified for the 1956 Summer Olympics in Melbourne, Australia, at the age of sixteen, but also won a bronze medal in the 4x100-metre relay race.

Four years later, Wilma returned to the Olympics in Rome, Italy. She had suffered a torn hamstring just a few months before the games and was told by doctors that she would not be able to compete. However, she refused to give up on her dream and continued to train with a special brace on her leg. In the end, Wilma not only competed, but also won three gold medals: in the 100-metre dash, the 200-metre dash and the 4x100-metre relay. She became the first American woman to win three gold medals in track and field at a single Olympic Games.

Wilma Rudolph's story is a testament to the power of perseverance in the face of adversity. Despite being told "no" repeatedly by doctors and others, she refused to give up on her dreams and went on to achieve greatness. Her legacy continues to inspire people around the world to this day.

Benefits of teamwork

Success is not always a solo pursuit; it is a collaborative effort that requires the collective effort of individuals working together towards a common goal. This is particularly evident in our fast-paced and competitive world, where teamwork has emerged as a vital component for success across sports, business and various domains.

Collaborative endeavours empower different individuals to bring together their distinct skills, knowledge and resources towards a shared goal, helping them to surmount challenges and achieve greatness. Teamwork not only magnifies problem-solving abilities, but also nurtures a sense of unity and camaraderie among members. A shared purpose fosters commitment and a positive work atmosphere, where each individual feels valued.

Teamwork as a practice also ensures an equitable distribution of tasks. This allows members of a team to capitalize on their strengths while compensating for weaknesses, enhancing overall efficiency and productivity.

Nevertheless, effective teamwork demands open communication, active listening, flexibility and mutual trust. It mandates supporting each other through triumphs and setbacks, holding specific roles and embracing accountability. Though demanding, teamwork has its definite benefits: united resources, camaraderie and efficient workload distribution. These far surpass the challenges of working as a team. Embracing the ethos of teamwork leads individuals towards excellence and collective accomplishments.

Who has not heard of landing on the moon? Recent successes of India's space programme have reignited the prospect of moon landing in our imagination. But we should never forget how such missions have always been the paragon of teamwork and collaborative achievement.

Take NASA's *Apollo 11* mission, which achieved the historic first moon landing on 20 July 1969. Neil Armstrong is the one individual we remember most from that endeavour, but the mission showcased remarkable coordination among thousands of individuals, including scientists, engineers and astronauts. The mission used the expertise of professionals from diverse fields such as aerospace engineering, physics, mathematics and computer science. This interdisciplinary collaboration was instrumental in designing, constructing and operating the spacecraft and its associated systems. Every team member had well-defined roles and responsibilities. Astronauts were tasked with lunar exploration, while mission control personnel meticulously monitored spacecraft systems from earth. Astronauts maintained constant contact with mission control, while various teams on earth shared critical information and made real-time decisions. Every contributor to the Apollo programme shared a singular mission: landing humans on the moon safely and returning them to earth. This shared purpose galvanized the team, fostering unity and dedication.

The triumphant moon landing of *Apollo 11* serves as an iconic illustration of how effective teamwork, collaboration and unwavering commitment to a collective goal can yield monumental achievements.

Measuring the fruit of hard work

Achieving success is often considered to be the ultimate goal of hard work, dedication and perseverance. But what does success really mean? Is it merely achieving wealth, fame or power? Or is it a more nuanced concept that varies from person to person? How do we know if we are successful? How can we measure the fruit of our hard work?

The truth is, success can be defined in multiple ways, and what constitutes success for one individual might not be the same for another. For some, success could mean reaching the pinnacle of their career, while for others, it could mean being able to balance work and personal life. Some may see success as achieving financial stability, while others may see it as being in a position of power or authority. Still others may measure their success through how many great adventures they have had in their lives!

Therefore, how we will measure success is a highly subjective matter and it depends largely on our personal goals, values and aspirations. However, there is no denying that there exist certain universal indicators which can help us gauge our success, regardless of our personal definitions. What are they?

Goal achievement

One of the simplest ways to measure the success of our hard work is by evaluating whether or not we have achieved the goals that we set for ourselves. If we have accomplished our objectives, our hard work has been successful.

Progression

Another way to measure the success of our hard work is by evaluating the amount of progress we have made towards achieving our goals. Even if we have not completed our tasks yet and arrived at our ideal place, if we have made significant progress then our hard work has paid off.

Financial competence

In some cases, financial rewards can also be an indicator of success. If our hard work has led to a promotion, raise or increased income, that can be a sign that we are successful in our career.

Feedback

Feedback from others can be a useful tool in measuring the success of our hard work. If the feedback is positive and constructive, we can be confident that our hard work has been successful.

Personal satisfaction

Ultimately, the success of our hard work should be measured by how satisfied we are with the results—and with ourselves. If we are happy with what we have achieved and comfortable with where we are, our hard work has been fruitful, regardless of whether or not others agree.

Conclusion

Since success is a coveted goal, everyone pursues it through means that suit them. Yet, it is unequivocally clear that there are no quick routes to success despite tempting promises of effortless triumphs. The allure of shortcuts is strong, and it is fuelled by a modern society saturated with messages of rapid success. These pledges suggest that prosperity can be easily acquired without hard work.

However, genuine success needs unwavering commitment, diligence and persistence. It comes from consistent effort, which involves goal-setting, meticulous planning and unflagging work. While shortcuts may offer seemingly quick victories, they often entail negative repercussions in the long term. Relying on shortcuts can breed complacency, undermining of genuine effort and motivation, resulting in incomplete undertakings, errors and even, in the end, failure.

In contrast, hard work fosters deep comprehension of tasks and innovative and effective solutions. It also nurtures resilience, a key asset for overcoming challenges. Real success surpasses mere material achievements, for it includes personal development, self-betterment and the gratification that comes from strenuous yet meaningful accomplishments. It shows that the journey towards success is as important as the destination.

The truth therefore is that shortcuts do not lead to success. While often overshadowed by a culture of instant gratification, the path to accomplishment requires perseverance and sacrifices. Whether it is personal or professional success, only those willing to put in genuine hard work stand a realistic chance of attaining success. And that is why hard work is one of the foundational principles of the 8-H way of life.

3
Hobby

> "The creative adult is the child who survived."
> —Ursula K. Le Guin

Now, how many times have we heard the proverb, All work and no play makes Jack a dull boy? While hard work is the bedrock of success, what we do outside of work is equally important if we are to lead a balanced, fulfilling, happy life. The two chapters that follow strategically delve into the significance of "play".

I once knew a young man named Aatish who was going through a difficult time in his life. He had just lost his job, had broken up with his partner, and was feeling lost and uncertain about his future. Aatish felt overwhelmed and hopeless, and he did not know how to cope with his emotions.

One day, Aatish stumbled upon an art-supplies store while walking in his neighbourhood. He had always enjoyed art while in school but never bothered to pursue it as a grown-up. The pressures of crafting a "conventional" career had made him forget about his childhood passion. Now, drawn by the colourful paints and empty canvases, he decided to buy some supplies and give it a try.

At first, Aatish struggled with the basic techniques and felt frustrated. But he did not give up. Instead, he looked up numerous YouTube videos to develop his skills. He clung to his art, pouring all his emotions onto the canvas. As he continued to paint, he found that he was able to express his emotions and thoughts in a way that he could not with words. He started to see the beauty in imperfection too. He found that his hobby had become much more than just a way to pass the time. His passion for art was something that he could hold on to, no matter what challenges came his way.

Aatish began to paint every day, even if it was just for a few minutes. He discovered that the act of creating something with his hands was incredibly therapeutic, and his spirit began to lift. He realized that with time he could better manage his anxiety and depression as well. He began sharing his artwork with others on social media and received praise and encouragement, which helped boost his self-esteem.

And then, something miraculous happened. Aatish's artwork caught the attention of a local gallery owner, and he was invited to exhibit his paintings in a group art show. The exhibition was a huge success, and Aatish's work in the show received special attention and admiration. He was amazed by such positive response. The news of his talent spread, and soon Aatish was given solo shows not only at the same gallery but also at art centres in other cities.

Aatish's hobby, which was once just a passion and a way to alleviate pain, became his profession, and his life took a decisive turn. As he painted more, his paintings became more expressive, experimental and exquisite. His art touched the hearts of viewers and received ample praise from art critics, making him a valuable member of the art fraternity.

Aatish's hobby not only saved him from his darkest days, but also gave him a new purpose and direction in life. His talent and perseverance helped him overcome his struggles. And most importantly, it made him happy.

The healing power of hobbies

Today, especially after the world has struggled through a debilitating pandemic, there is a newfound appreciation for the simple joys of life. One of these joys is the pursuit of hobbies, which has been revealed as an essential aspect of human existence. Hobbies are not mere distractions or time-fillers, but rather a vital part of our mental and emotional well-being. They allow us to explore our creativity, express our passions and learn new skills. Hobbies also offer a sense of accomplishment and satisfaction, which can be especially valuable during challenging times.

Hobbies provide numerous benefits to human lives. First and foremost, hobbies provide us with a sense of purpose. Having something that we are passionate about and actively working towards can give us a sense of direction in life. Let us now explore the numerous benefits of hobbies and why everyone should have at least one.

Physical health benefits of pursuing a hobby

Reduces stress

Stress and anxiety can contribute to several health issues, including high blood pressure, heart disease and obesity. By engaging in a hobby, we can take our mind off our worries and focus on something that we enjoy, which can lead to reduced levels of the stress hormone cortisol.

Boosts immune system

Studies have shown that positive emotions can increase the production of antibodies, which can help fight off infections. Hobbies, such as painting, playing an instrument or gardening, can help increase our levels of happiness and positive emotions, which can in turn boost our immune system.

Improves fine motor skills

Fine motor skills refer to the ability to control small muscles in the hands and fingers, allowing for precise movements and dexterity. When pursuing a hobby that involves fine motor skills, individuals must repeatedly perform small, coordinated movements with their hands and fingers. This repetitive practice can help to strengthen the muscles and improve their control and coordination. For example, playing a musical instrument and painting, drawing and sculpting require control over small movements of the hand and fingers.

Mental health benefits of pursuing a hobby

Promotes mindfulness

When we engage in a hobby, we are fully immersed in the activity. We are not thinking about the past or worrying about the future—we are focused on the present moment. This kind of absorption is similar to what happens when we are in a state of "flow", a term coined by psychologist Mihaly Csikszentmihalyi to describe the experience of being completely involved in an activity to the point where everything else fades away. Being in a state of flow can be incredibly restorative. Studies have shown that engaging in activities that promote flow can be just as effective at reducing stress as traditional mindfulness practices like meditation.

Increases self-esteem

Self-esteem is a crucial aspect of mental health that influences how we feel about our abilities, worth and potential for success.

Low self-esteem can lead to negative thinking patterns, self-doubt and a lack of motivation. But engaging in hobbies helps us boost our self-esteem. How?

By creating a sense of accomplishment: Hobbies allow us to set goals, work towards them and achieve them. This sense of accomplishment provides a sense of pride in our abilities.

By attracting positive feedback: Getting praise or recognition for our skills from peers increases feelings of self-worth and validation.

By allowing creative expression: Hobbies allow us to express our creativity and individuality. Creating something unique can give us a sense of pride in ourselves and our abilities.

By moving us away from stress: Hobbies can serve as a healthy distraction from daily stressors, providing an escape from negative thoughts and low self-esteem.

By promoting new skills: Pursuing a hobby can involve learning new skills or acquiring new knowledge, providing a sense of mastery and a feeling of self-worth.

Provides a sense of community

If we are interested in, say, painting, we may join a local art group or take a painting class. By doing so, we will be surrounded by people who share our passion for art, and we can collaborate with other artists. Similarly, if we enjoy playing sports, joining a local sports team can be a great way to meet new people who share our love of the game. Whether we are playing basketball, soccer or tennis, being part of a team can create camaraderie and connection that extend beyond the playing field. Or, if we enjoy social work, joining a volunteer group can be a great way to connect with other people who share our desire to give back to the community. This sense of community is an important part of our overall mental well-being.

Strengthens relationships

Hobbies do not need to be individual pursuits. Engaging in hobbies with our partner or loved ones can have several benefits for our relationship. Joint recreational activities create shared memories and experiences that we can look back on and reminisce about. This helps strengthen our mutual bond. Pursuing hobbies together encourages open communication between partners, building trust. Mutual support in hobbies fosters teamwork and cooperation, which in turn enhances relationships. Finally, exploring hobbies together exposes new experiences, deepening connections and understanding.

The kaleidoscope of hobbies and their therapeutic values

Hobbies are kaleidoscopic expressions of human nature; they paint a rich and varied tapestry of our interests and passions. From the meditative stillness of a painter's brushstroke to the frenzied tempo of a dancer's footwork, hobbies offer a variety of experiences that enrich our lives. So, what are the many types of hobbies and the dazzling array of colours and textures they offer? Here are some categories:

Creative

Artistic pursuits like painting, writing and music, foster self-expression and emotional release.

Learning

Skill acquisition like cooking, coding and languages, enhance cognition and growth, which can be applied in our personal or professional life.

Outdoor

Nature-oriented hobbies such as camping, hiking and gardening promote fitness, tranquillity and learning about the environment.

Collecting

Gathering items like stamps, coins or art offers historical insights; these hobbies can also be a form of investment, as certain items appreciate in value over time.

Gaming

Playing video, board or card games provides entertainment enhances mental acuity and boosts problem-solving skills.

Active

Physical activities like sports and dancing boost fitness as well as social connections.

Social

Group endeavours like participating in book club discussions and volunteering forge connections and enhance well-being.

Travelling

Exploring new places and cultures creates memorable experiences and escapes from routine.

Resting

Activities like reading, meditation and napping promote mental and physical relaxation.

The art of choosing the perfect hobby

A hobby is not just a pastime; it can be a passion that fuels our soul with purpose and meaning. In the grand canvas of life, hobbies are the vibrant brushstrokes that bring colours and textures to what can be an otherwise plain existence. Therefore, choosing the right hobby is not just important but critical for our overall well-being.

Yet, like an artist searching for the perfect shade of blue, finding the right hobby can be a daunting task, especially if we are unsure of what we enjoy. There are countless options, each with its own appeal. The key is to approach the process with an open mind and a curious spirit. Here are a few tips:

Think about our larger goals and aspirations

What do we hope to achieve through our hobbies? Do we want to learn a new skill, meet new people or simply have fun? Understanding our goals can help us identify hobbies that align with our priorities.

Explore our interests and passions

What are the things that make us happy? What do we enjoy doing in our free time? It is important to make a list of our interests, skills and talents. This will give us an idea of what we might like to pursue further.

Consider our personality and lifestyle

What kind of person are we? What are our strengths and weaknesses? What are our time constraints and commitments? It is important to choose a hobby that aligns with our personality, values and lifestyle. Think about how much time we must devote to a hobby. If we have limited free time, we need to consider a hobby that can be done in short bursts, like reading or writing.

Be open-minded

It is important not to limit ourselves to our current interests. It is critical to experiment with different activities, and be open to learning and growing.

Consider the budget

Some hobbies can be expensive, while others can be done on a shoestring budget. It is important to consider how much money we are able and willing to invest in our hobby before deciding.

Do not be afraid to change

Remember that hobbies are meant to be enjoyable, so if we find that a particular hobby is not bringing us pleasure, do not be afraid to try something new.

Look for community

It might help to consider if there are hobby groups or clubs in our area. Joining a community of like-minded individuals can make our hobby more enjoyable and help us learn new skills.

Try before we commit

Before fully committing to a hobby, we must try it out on a small scale. Attending a class or workshop, borrowing equipment from a friend or joining a local club to see if it is really something we enjoy may help.

Start small

We should not try to do too much too soon. We could start with a small project or activity and gradually build up our skills and knowledge.

Ask for recommendations

Asking friends, family or co-workers about their hobbies and what they enjoy about them might help. They may have suggestions that we never thought of before.

With patience, curiosity and an open heart, we can find the perfect hobby that suits our unique personality and aspirations. So, let us go ahead, unleash our creativity and let our passions guide us to a world of infinite possibilities.

The role hobbies play in personal growth and development

> "The habits formed in childhood are often the ones that last a lifetime. Encouraging children to pursue hobbies from a young age can set them on a path of lifelong learning and personal fulfilment."—Melinda Gates

Dr Bobby Sager is a successful businessman, philanthropist and photographer who credits his love for photography as a child for much of his success. Sager grew up in a working-class family in Boston, Massachusetts. When he was just ten years old, he received a camera from his grandmother as a gift, which sparked a passion for photography in Sager that would last a lifetime.

As a young teenager, Sager would ride his bike to different neighbourhoods in Boston, taking pictures of everything he saw. He would spend hours in his darkroom, experimenting with developing techniques and creating prints. By the time he was in high school, Sager was selling his photographs to local businesses and newspapers.

Sager went on to attend college and pursued a successful career in business, but his passion for photography never waned. He continued to take pictures and developed a reputation as a talented photographer. His travels took him to destinations around the world, including Nepal, Tibet, Rwanda, Sudan, Haiti, Syria, Afghanistan, Iraq, Israel and Palestine. He captured stunning photographs of not only the sites, but also documented the daily struggle of people in these lands. Sager's photographic journey is a testament to the power of images to tell stories and bring attention to important issues around the world.

In addition to his business and photography careers, Sager has also become known for his philanthropic work. He has donated millions of dollars to various causes, including education and global health initiatives. He has also worked to promote peace and understanding in conflict zones around the world.

Sager attributes much of his success in life to his early love for photography. In interviews, he has spoken about how his hobby helped him develop important skills such as focus, patience and attention to detail. He also credits his photography with teaching him to see the world from different perspectives and to appreciate the beauty in everyday life.

Whether it is photography, music, writing or any other hobby, the benefits of starting early can be profound. These include developing valuable skills, a sense of identity, confidence, mental health, social connections, healthy habits and time management skills. By pursuing a hobby that they are passionate about, children and teenagers can learn new things, develop their talents and grow as individuals.

Hobbies of famous people—fictional, mythological, real life

Throughout history, famous individuals have indulged in hobbies, showcasing their diverse interests and talents. It might be argued that their pursuit of hobbies has been an important aspect of their all-round success in life.

In the realm of fiction, Sherlock Holmes was passionate about the violin, boxing and conducting chemical experiments. In mythology, Lord Krishna was renowned for his mastery of the flute and mesmerizing devotional singing. Arjuna embraced the flute, acquiring the skill from Lord Krishna himself. The demon king Ravana displayed a love for the veena, music and extensive Vedic knowledge.

Among prominent rulers, we can look at the famous monarchs of England. King Henry VIII's interests encompassed jousting, hunting and music. Elizabeth I, known for her vibrant reign, engaged in music, poetry and outdoor sports. Queen Elizabeth II's hobbies included horse racing and breeding, showcasing her deep connection with equestrian pursuits. Japanese Emperor Hirohito delved into marine biology and scientific contributions, enriching his intellectual pursuits and leaving a mark on science itself. Julius Caesar left a mark through his writings and historical accounts, preserving his legacy for all eternity.

Among political leaders, Barack Obama revels in basketball, golf, music and reading. Angela Merkel finds solace in hiking and classical music. Justin Trudeau has been known to embrace outdoor activities like snowboarding, kayaking and even boxing. Jacinda Ardern enjoys hiking, cooking and playing the guitar, reflecting her well-rounded interests. Vladimir Putin showcases his physical prowess through judo and ice hockey. Cyril Ramaphosa explores the great outdoors through fly-fishing, photography and running. Sheikh Hasina indulges in cooking, gardening and cultivating orchids. Sheikh Mohammed bin Rashid Al Maktoum, Vice President and Prime Minister of the United Arab Emirates, channels his passion into horse breeding and racing. Aung San Suu Kyi finds joy in gardening, reading and classical music. And Mahathir Mohamad expresses his artistic side through photography.

These icons exemplify the richness and diversity of human interests. They reveal the profound impact hobbies can have on shaping individual lives and legacies.

The challenges of pursuing a hobby and how to overcome them

While pursuing a hobby, individuals may face various challenges that can hinder their progress. Here are some of the most common challenges one might face and how to overcome them:

Lack of time

Often, we find ourselves juggling multiple commitments, including work, family and social obligations, which leave little room for pursuing our interests. It can be challenging to carve out time for hobbies, especially if they require a significant investment of time and effort.

To overcome this challenge, we should start by effectively managing time: set realistic goals and build a structured schedule for our hobby. Allocate specific time slots, like dedicating evenings or weekends, to pursue our passion. Next, integrate our hobby into daily routines. For example, we can listen to audiobooks during commutes or set up a home art studio for brief daily painting sessions. Stay disciplined and committed, and maintain consistent practice even in short moments. Prioritizing time, dedication and steady effort will enable us to successfully incorporate our hobby into our lives.

Financial constraints

Many hobbies can be expensive and may require specialized equipment or supplies that can be costly. The cost of classes or workshops can also add up quickly. This can make it difficult if we have limited financial resources to pursue our passions.

To overcome such financial barriers in our pursuit of hobbies, we need to adopt strategies like budgeting and allocating resources to meet our hobby needs while reducing other expenses. Or opt for cost-effective alternatives, such as purchasing used supplies or attending affordable classes. It might be a good idea to seek community groups or free workshops for budget-friendly engagement.

Furthermore, monetization can be a useful option—selling crafts, teaching or providing hobby-related services over time can offset costs. Start modestly and increase investment gradually. Generating income from the hobby, through sales or services, also aids funding. In short, overcoming financial constraints involves thoughtful budgeting, economical choices and exploring income avenues to sustain and enjoy hobbies.

Lack of motivation

Hobbies often require a considerable amount of patience, dedication and practice if we want to become proficient in them. It can be challenging to stay motivated when progress seems slow. The temptation to give up and move on to something else can be strong in such a situation, especially if the hobby was initially taken up for relaxation or stress relief.

Overcoming such challenges involves various strategies. To start with, we should address the lack of progress by setting smaller, achievable goals, celebrating achievements, however small, and not being too hard on ourselves. Altering routines or exploring new approaches, such as trying different mediums in painting, for example, can help combat boredom. Avoid comparing your progress with others by focusing on self-improvement rather than competition. It is always important to take breaks, prioritize relaxation and maintain a fun perspective.

Sometimes, it can be hard to stay motivated when we are the only one holding ourselves accountable. We can counter this by partnering with a hobby buddy or joining a supportive community. Ultimately, sustaining motivation in hobbies hinges on preserving enjoyment and recalling the initial purpose—be it unwinding, creative expression or personal fulfilment. Adapting techniques to individual challenges helps cultivate a lasting and enriching hobby experience.

Social isolation

Hobbies are often solitary pursuits, requiring us to work on our own for long periods of time as they may be individual activities that do not require interaction with others. While this can be a great way to focus and achieve a sense of accomplishment, it can also be lonely and isolating, especially if our friends or family members do not share the same passion. Also, some hobbies require a lot of time and effort, which can make it difficult for people to socialize with others while pursuing their hobbies. For example, someone who spends a lot of time practising a musical instrument may have less time available to spend with friends and family.

But this challenge can also be overcome. We can join a club or group related to our hobby, allowing ourselves to connect with others who share our interests. Participate in activities that combine the hobby with socializing—for example, a writing group or a gaming night with friends.

Lack of space

Lack of space can be a significant challenge when pursuing a hobby. Depending on the hobby, space limitations may manifest in different ways. For example, a painter may need a large, well-ventilated space to store and use materials such as canvases, paint and brushes, while a musician may require a dedicated area for playing instruments and recording equipment.

Overcoming space limitations requires creative problem-solving and strategic planning. We need to prioritize our hobby's key elements, focusing on efficient storage if space is tight, or seeking room to move if necessary. Optimize existing space by organizing tools and materials, employing wall-mounted storage, or multi-purpose furniture. Explore unconventional spaces like community centres, co-working areas or outdoor venues to pursue our hobby.

We could also consider simplifying our hobby to minimize spatial requirements—try indoor gardening or downsized versions. There is ingenuity in sharing resources with fellow enthusiasts. We can collaborate on equipment, or repurposing underutilized areas. Through inventive thinking and adaptable strategies, we can ensure an enjoyable and fulfilling hobby experience.

Stepping out of our comfort zone

Stepping out of one's comfort zone is a common challenge when pursuing a new hobby, as it often requires venturing into unfamiliar territory and facing potential obstacles that may be daunting or even intimidating. However, breaking out of one's comfort zone can also lead to growth and new opportunities.

Fear of failure is a prevailing challenge. We can combat this by acknowledging failure's role in learning. Again, set achievable goals, and focus on progress and enjoyment rather than perfection. Being a beginner can be discomforting. To overcome this, we can seek a supportive community, like clubs, classes or online forums, for shared guidance and experiences. Adapting to change, another challenge, requires us to take intentional steps like scheduling hobby time or integrating it into existing routines. Embracing the discomfort of the unfamiliar can lead to personal development and open doors to novel experiences, highlighting the value of stepping outside comfort zones during hobby pursuits.

Conclusion

Believe it or not, hobbies can be a valuable tool for professional growth and development. First and foremost, hobbies can help us develop new skills and knowledge that can be transferred to our professional life. For example, if we enjoy woodworking as a hobby, we may learn how to use different tools, understand the properties of various types of wood and develop a keen eye for detail. These skills can easily be applied to other areas of our life, such as a job that requires attention to detail, problem-solving or creativity.

Similarly, hobbies can help us build a network of people with similar interests. This network can be invaluable for professional networking and can lead to opportunities that we may not have otherwise been exposed to. For instance, if we enjoy photography as a hobby, we may meet other photographers who can introduce us to potential clients or job opportunities.

Pursuing a hobby can also help us develop important soft skills, such as time management, organization and discipline. These skills are highly valued by employers and can help us stand out in a competitive job market. For example, if we enjoy running as a hobby, we may develop a routine of waking up early to train, tracking our progress and setting goals for ourselves. These habits can be easily applied to our professional life, helping us stay focused and productive.

Another way hobbies can help our career is by introducing us to new experiences. For example, if we love to travel, we may also have a natural curiosity and openness to new ideas and cultures. This trait can be beneficial in any industry, as it allows us to approach challenges with a fresh perspective and come up with creative solutions.

Various successful individuals credit their hobbies for shaping their accomplishments. Sara Blakely's stand-up comedy experience fostered communication skills and confidence which proved pivotal for pitching Spanx to investors. Elon Musk's early love for science fiction fuelled his engineering and space exploration pursuits. Similarly, Richard Branson's adventurous spirit facilitated calculated risk-taking and business success. Mark Zuckerberg's middle school coding hobby evolved into Facebook's historic creation. Stephen King's hobby of creative writing as a teacher transformed into an illustrious career as a bestselling author. Cooking was merely a hobby for chef Thomas Keller, but eventually it led to him owning world-renowned restaurants. Tennis legend Serena Williams' fashion designing has complemented her career in sport.

In short, hobbies can profoundly shape successful paths by bridging creativity, skills and determination. So, if we already have a hobby, we need to cultivate it further. If not, we should choose one and make it a part of our life.

4 HOLIDAY

> "The joy of life comes from our encounters with new experiences, and hence there is no greater joy than to have an endlessly changing horizon, for each day to have a new and different sun." —Jon Krakauer

I once knew a man named Rajeev who was a workaholic. He was a successful businessman, working long hours every day, including weekends. He believed that working all the time was the only way to be successful and that taking breaks or holidays was a waste of time.

One day, Rajeev fell ill and had to take a month off work. During that time, he realized that his health had suffered due to his workaholic lifestyle. He had developed high blood pressure, anxiety and depression. His doctor advised him to go on a holiday to reduce his stress levels and improve his health. Rajeev reluctantly agreed and went on a two-week vacation to a beach resort.

During his vacation, Rajeev realized how much he had been missing out on life. He spent his days relaxing on the beach, reading books he had always meant to read and exploring the town learning about the local culture. He enjoyed spending time with his family and he felt a sense of peace that he had not felt in years.

When Rajeev returned to work, he was a changed man. He no longer worked long hours, and he made sure to take breaks and holidays regularly. He realized that taking time off was not a waste but essential to his mental and physical well-being. Rajeev's business also improved because of his new approach to work. He was more productive and efficient, and he found that his employees were happier and more motivated when he took breaks and encouraged them to do the same.

As the pace of life continues to accelerate, it can be easy to get caught up in a cycle of non-stop activity and forget the importance of taking breaks and time off. Also, we often take pride in our ability to work tirelessly for extended periods of time. We see it as a badge of honour to work long hours, skip lunch breaks and push ourselves to our limits. However, what we fail to recognize is that such behaviour is not sustainable and can be detrimental to our overall well-being.

Benefits of taking short breaks

> "Almost everything will work again if you unplug it for a few minutes—including you."—Anne Lamott

Research has shown that taking short breaks every ninety minutes can improve focus and creativity. Our brains need time to recharge, and by taking a break, we allow our minds to rest and replenish. Short breaks can take many forms, such as going for a walk, grabbing a cup of coffee or simply taking a few deep breaths. These activities help to reduce stress, increase motivation and prevent the onset of mental exhaustion.

While taking daily breaks is essential, it is equally important to take more extended breaks in the form of vacations or holidays. Holidays provide an opportunity to disconnect from work, unwind and recharge. Research has shown that taking vacations can help reduce stress, improve sleep quality and increase overall life satisfaction. Furthermore, holidays allow us to step outside our daily routines and have new experiences. Whether it is exploring a new city, trying out new cuisines or learning about a different culture, vacations provide an opportunity for personal growth and development.

In this chapter, we will explore the value of taking short breaks as well as longer holidays and discuss the many aspects of this important pillar of the 8-H Principle.

But first, let us summarize the benefits of taking short breaks:

Increased productivity

Taking regular breaks throughout the day can help us stay focused and productive. It allows our brains to recharge, leading to improved concentration and better decision-making.

Reduced stress

Breaks can help reduce the production of stress hormones like cortisol and adrenaline. By taking breaks, we allow our body's stress response system to settle, promoting a sense of calm.

Improved physical health

Sitting for long periods can lead to various health problems such as back pain, eye strain and poor posture. Taking short breaks for exercise, stretching, strolls or other movements can help reduce the risk of these health problems.

Better mental health

Taking breaks can help improve our mental health by reducing anxiety, depression and similar or related issues.

Stronger relationships

Holidays can provide an opportunity to strengthen relationships with our friends and family. It allows us to spend quality time with our loved ones, creating memories and deepening connections.

Enhanced creativity

Stepping away from our work can help us be more creative. When we take a break, we give our minds a chance to wander, which can lead to new ideas and insights.

How to go about scheduling short breaks

Planning short breaks in advance and making them a regular part of our daily routine is a great strategy to ensure that we take breaks and recharge ourselves. Here are some tips to help us plan our breaks effectively:

Identify our priorities

We need to start by identifying what is important to us and what activities help us relax and unwind. This can be anything from reading a book to going for a walk in the park or spending time with our friends and family.

Set realistic goals

Once we know what we want to do with our free time, we should set realistic goals for ourselves. This means thinking about how much time we can realistically take off each day, and what we can realistically achieve in that time.

Schedule breaks into our calendar

Just like we schedule appointments and meetings, we need to schedule our breaks into our calendar so that we have a specific time and duration set aside for relaxation.

Decide the length of our breaks

We should decide on the length of our breaks based on our schedule and the amount of time we need to rest and recharge. We can take short breaks of 5–10 minutes every hour or little longer breaks every few hours.

Plan our activities

We must plan what we want to do during our breaks. This can be anything from going for a walk, meditating, reading or simply taking a power nap. Having a plan will make it easier for us to stick to our break schedule.

Minimize distractions

When it is time for our daily break, we should try to minimize distractions as much as possible. This might mean turning off our phone or email notifications, or finding a quiet spot where we will not be disturbed.

Be flexible

While it is good to stick to our schedule, it is also important to be flexible. If something unexpected comes up, or if we are not feeling all right with a certain activity, we should not hesitate to adjust our plans.

Stay committed

Finally, remember that taking short breaks is an important part of self-care, and it is something that we should be committed to over the long term. So even if we have a busy day or things do not go according to plan, we need to make sure we find time for ourselves daily.

A deep dive into the cost of constant distraction

Distractions can be a significant cause of stress in our lives. When we are constantly interrupted by notifications and messages, we can become overwhelmed and feel like we are always playing catch-up. This constant feeling of being behind can cause us to feel stressed and anxious, leading to a decrease in our overall well-being.

To begin with, it is important to understand how distractions affect our brains. Our brains are wired to seek out novelty and respond to new information. When we are exposed to a new stimulus, our brains release dopamine, a neurotransmitter that gives us a sense of pleasure and reward. This is why it is so easy to get sucked into a social media feed or lose track of time while browsing the internet.

However, while distractions may provide temporary pleasure, they can have long-term negative consequences. Studies have shown that people who are frequently interrupted by distractions have higher levels of the stress hormone cortisol in their system, leading to an increased risk of developing health problems such as heart disease and diabetes.

In addition to causing stress, distractions also lead to a lack of quality in both our professional and personal lives. When we are constantly switching between tasks, we never fully engage with any one thing. This can lead to a decrease in the quality of our work, as well as our relationships. For example, if we are constantly checking our phone during a conversation with a friend, we miss important details of the conversation or fail to fully engage with them. This leads to a lack of meaningful connection and a decreased sense of fulfilment in our lives.

Distractions can also impact our ability to achieve our goals. When we are constantly interrupted, it can be difficult to stay focused on what we truly want to accomplish. We may find ourselves getting side-tracked by other tasks, leading to a lack of progress towards our goals and a feeling of being stuck in our lives.

How to remain present in a distracted world

Ubiquitous technology has brought with it an endless stream of notifications, pop-ups and alerts that compete for our attention, making it harder than ever to concentrate on the task at hand. Whether we are studying, working or simply relaxing, distractions can hinder our ability to perform our best. The first step is to recognize the distractions in our lives and be mindful of how they affect us. Then, apply these strategies to effectively manage distraction:

Minimize external distraction

One of the most effective ways to manage distraction is to reduce the number of external stimuli that compete for our attention. This can be done by:
- Turning off notifications on our phone, computer or other electronic devices
- Closing unnecessary tabs on our browsers or applications
- Creating a quiet, clutter-free workspace

For example, if we are working on a project that requires our full attention, we need to turn off our phone or put it on silent mode. This will prevent us from being distracted by incoming messages or notifications.

Use time-management techniques

Another effective strategy to manage distraction is to use time-management techniques. This involves breaking our work or study sessions into smaller, manageable tasks and scheduling specific times for each task. For example, if we have a project that is due in two weeks, we must break it down into smaller tasks and schedule specific times for each task. This will help us stay focused and avoid procrastination.

Practise mindfulness

Mindfulness is the practice of being fully present and engaged in the moment. It can help us manage distraction by training our mind to focus on one thing at a time. Mindfulness can be practised through meditation, deep breathing or simply by paying attention to our surroundings. For example, if we find ourselves getting distracted while working, take a few deep breaths and focus on our breathing. This will help calm our mind and bring us back to the present moment.

Create a distraction-free environment

Creating a distraction-free environment is also important. This may mean finding a quiet workspace, if possible, where we can work without interruptions, or investing in noise-cancelling headphones. We should also de-clutter our workspace, arranging essential things properly on our desk and removing any item that could distract us.

Benefits of taking a digital break

> "Life is messy and complicated, and that's what makes it beautiful." —Demi Lovato

Madison Holleran was a nineteen-year-old promising young student at the University of Pennsylvania. She was a talented track-and-field athlete who had always excelled in both academics and sports. She had a supportive family. She was also a popular and outgoing young woman who seemed to have everything going for her. She had a large following on Instagram, of what appeared to be a perfect life. However, behind the facade, Madison was struggling with anxiety and depression.

On 17 January 2014, Madison took her own life by jumping from the roof of a parking garage in Philadelphia. Her death shocked her family, friends and the entire community of her university. It was only after her death that her family and friends discovered the true extent of her inner struggles.

In the aftermath of her death, it became clear that Madison was under tremendous pressure to maintain her perfect image on social media. She had been comparing herself to others on Instagram and Facebook and felt like she could never measure up to their seemingly perfect lives. She had also been struggling with the pressure to perform well both academically and athletically and felt like she was failing in both areas.

Madison's tragic story is a powerful reminder of the dangers of portraying a perfect life online. In today's world dominated by social media, the pressure to appear happy has never been greater. Every day, we scroll through countless images of people smiling, laughing and seemingly living their best lives. The message is clear: if you are unhappy, there must be something wrong with you. People may start to believe that everyone around them is leading a perfect life while only they are struggling.

Unfortunately, this pressure to present a facade of happiness is affecting people of all ages, backgrounds and cultures. It is the reason why we feel compelled to post pictures of ourselves at parties, on vacation or with our significant others, whether or not we are happy in those moments. It is the reason why we constantly compare ourselves to others, measuring our own happiness against the seemingly perfect lives of our peers.

But what is the cost of this obsession with happiness? Is it worth sacrificing our authenticity and our vulnerability for the sake of a perfect image? What happens when we can no longer keep up the charade, when the weight of our own expectations becomes too heavy to bear?

The truth is that the pressure to be happy is not just unhealthy, it is also unsustainable. It is impossible to be happy all the time, and yet we continue to strive for a state of perpetual bliss, chasing an ideal that can never be fully realized. In our quest for happiness, we lose sight of the beauty and complexity of life, of the moments of sadness, anger and frustration that make us who we are. It is important for us to remember that social media is just a highlight reel of people's lives, and that we should never compare ourselves to others based on what we see online.

Embracing our imperfections

In his book *The Happiness Trap*, psychologist Russ Harris argues that the pursuit of happiness is often counterproductive, leading to feelings of disappointment and inadequacy. Instead, he suggests that we focus on building a rich, meaningful life, one that encompasses both positive and negative experiences.

This approach is echoed by the Danish concept of *hygge*, which celebrates the small, cosy moments of life regardless of whether they are happy or sad. *Hygge reminds us that happiness is not a destination, but rather a journey, one that is filled with both joy and sorrow.*

But how do we break free from the pressure to be happy? It starts with recognizing that the images we see on social media are not the reality. They are carefully curated and edited versions of people's lives, designed to present a certain image. We must learn to separate our own happiness from the happiness of others, to accept that we are all different, with unique struggles and challenges.

What if we embrace imperfection instead? What if we allow ourselves to be vulnerable and real online? What if we share our struggles and our failures along with our successes? What if we celebrated our authentic selves, rather than trying to conform to an impossible standard?

Some of the most popular influencers on social media today are those who are unapologetically themselves. They share their flaws, their fears and their failures, and in doing so, they connect with their audiences in a meaningful way. They show that it is okay to be imperfect, and that true happiness comes from embracing our authentic selves.

In the words of the poet Rumi, "The wound is the place where the light enters you." Our struggles and our pain are not something to be ashamed of, but rather a source of strength and growth. By embracing our imperfections, we can create a more meaningful, fulfilling life, one that is grounded in authenticity and self-acceptance.

> "Unplugging is not about denying ourselves the pleasures of technology. It's about discovering our true selves and the pleasures of the real world." —Chris Raine

In this digital age, we are glued to our screens, scrolling endlessly, consuming information and staying connected to our social circles. Our addiction to technology has become so severe that it is difficult to imagine our lives without it. But how often do we think about the impact it has on our mental and physical health?

That is where a holiday from the digital comes into play. Digital detox is a conscious decision to disconnect from technology and the internet, even for a short period of time. By disconnecting from our devices, we create space to breathe, think, feel and connect. Hence, a digital detox is not just about disconnecting from technology; it is also about connecting with ourselves and the world around us. We can use this time to read a book, take a walk, appreciate the beauty of Nature or simply sit in silence and reflect on our lives.

Additionally, a digital detox can help improve our sleep. The blue light emitted by our devices can disrupt our sleep patterns. By turning it off, we allow our minds to unwind and prepare for a peaceful night's sleep. It also helps to improve our relationships. When we are constantly distracted by our devices, we miss out on opportunities to connect with the people around us. By disconnecting from technology, we can focus on building deeper human connections and truly being present in the moment.

How to take out me-time

Amid our daily chaos, we often find ourselves longing for a moment of solitude, a moment to catch our breath and reconnect with ourselves. This moment is often referred to as "me-time", a sacred space where we can let go of the noise and distractions of the world and simply be.

Me-time is a time for self-reflection. It is a time to confront the fears and doubts that we often push aside in our daily lives. In this space, we can connect with our innermost selves and find the clarity and perspective we need to navigate life's challenges. It is a reminder that we are worthy of our own time and attention.

But me-time is not just a luxury; it is a necessity. Me-time is a vital aspect of our lives, and we should strive to make it a priority. It is a reminder that we are not just human *doings*, but human *beings*, and that our worth is not measured only by our productivity, but also by our very existence.

What is more, me-time is not just about taking a break from the world, but also about discovering new passions and unlocking hidden talents. Perhaps you have always wanted to learn how to play the guitar or try your hand at calligraphy. Now is the time to take that first step, to let your curiosity guide you and to embrace the unknown. In the process, you may discover a whole new world that you never knew existed. The poet Mary Oliver once wrote, "Tell me, what is it you plan to do with your one wild and precious life?"

Me-time is the space where we can answer that question.

In a world that often values busyness over stillness, *me-time is a radical act of self-love*. But me-time is not always easy to come by. It requires us to set boundaries, to say no to the demands of others and yes to our own needs. It requires us to prioritize ourselves and our well-being, even in the face of societal pressures to do otherwise.

So, if we are feeling overwhelmed and in need of some me-time, we need to take a deep breath and remember that we are worthy of this space. It may not always be easy to come by, but it is always worth the effort.

So, how can we prioritize this crucial aspect of self-care in our daily routine? The answer lies in the art of strategy.

Include me-time in our daily schedule

By intentionally designing our daily routine to incorporate moments of solitude and introspection, we can ensure that we get the much-needed me-time to recharge and refresh our mind and body. This could be as simple as scheduling a lunch break or a workout session. Or it could be a more extended time slot, such as an hour or two in the morning or evening.

Alter our daily routine

Consider waking up an hour earlier than usual to enjoy a cup of coffee in solitude, or taking a break away from our desk during the day to go for a walk.

Set boundaries and inform our loved ones

Remember that we can also set boundaries with our loved ones, letting them know that we need some alone time to recharge. Whatever works best for us, we need to stick to it and treat it as a non-negotiable commitment.

Find out what nourishes us

It is essential to identify the activities that nourish and replenish us. For some, it might be reading a book, practising yoga or taking a long bath. For others, it could be painting, listening to music or writing in a journal. It is important to find out what makes our heart sing and make it a regular part of our routine.

Create a sacred space

Another strategy is to create a sacred space in our home where we can relax. This could be a cosy corner with a comfortable chair, a yoga mat or a meditation pillow. We can fill the space with items that bring us joy and inspire us, such as books, art or music. Make it a haven that we look forward to visiting each day.

Change our mindset

The most crucial aspect of ensuring me-time in our daily routine is our mindset. We must shift our perspective from viewing self-care as a luxury to seeing it as a necessity. We must recognize that taking care of ourselves is not selfish but rather a prerequisite for being able to show up fully for others.

How to harness self-talk and its benefits

> "Talk to yourself like you would to someone you love."
> —Brené Brown

One of the preoccupations of me-time is self-talk—the inner dialogue or ongoing conversation that individuals have with themselves in their minds. Often when we are alone, we talk a lot to ourselves. This is an important part of our being in the world. In a society that can often be harsh and unforgiving, we have to be kind to ourselves.

So how can we harness the benefits of positive self-talk? Here are some practical strategies:

Use affirmations

Affirmations are positive statements that we can repeat to ourselves to help build our self-confidence and self-esteem, such as "I am capable of achieving my goals" or "I am worthy of love and respect".

Reframe negative thoughts

If we find ourselves thinking "I can't do this", reframe it to "I may find this challenging, but I am capable of figuring it out". Negative thoughts often creep into our mind, but we can reframe them in a more positive light.

Being kind to ourselves

It is imperative to treat ourselves with kindness and understanding. Rather than beating ourselves up for mistakes, acknowledge them and use them as opportunities for growth and learning.

Visualize achieving our goals

We need to picture ourselves achieving our goals and imagine the feelings of success and accomplishment. This can serve as motivation for us.

Practise gratitude

When we take a few moments each day to reflect on what we are thankful for in our lives, this will help us retain a positive mindset.

Surround ourselves with positivity

When we spend time with people who uplift us and engage in activities that make us feel good about ourselves, it reinforces positive self-talk and builds our confidence.

Exercise

Physical exercise releases endorphins, which are natural chemicals in our brain that promote feelings of happiness and positivity. When we exercise regularly, we may notice an improvement in our mood and self-esteem. This can lead to more positive self-talk, as we start to view ourselves in a more positive light.

Perform deep breathing

When we are feeling stressed, anxious or overwhelmed, our self-talk is generally negative. Deep-breathing exercises help us relax and reduce stress levels. Through them, we can calm our mind and body, which leads to more positive self-talk.

When to engage in self-talk

Positive self-talk is a powerful tool that can help us build confidence, reduce anxiety and increase motivation. But when is the best time to engage in this practice? The answer to this question is not simple, as there are different times that can be beneficial for different individuals. However, there are a few factors to consider when deciding when to engage in positive self-talk.

When we will not be distracted

Whether it is early in the morning or late at night, we need to choose a moment when we can be alone with our thoughts. This will allow us to focus on our inner voice without any external interruptions.

When we are in a positive and relaxed state of mind

It can be challenging to engage in self-encouragement when we are feeling overwhelmed or stressed. So it is crucial to find a moment when we are feeling calm and centred. This can be during a yoga session, a meditation practice or simply after taking a few deep breaths.

When considering our goals for the day

We might find it helpful to engage in positive self-talk before tackling a challenging task or making an important decision. Or it might work better if we reflect on our achievements at the end of the day, acknowledging our progress and celebrating our accomplishments.

Overall, there is no single right time to engage in positive self-talk. It is up to us to experiment and find the time that works best for us. However, here are some suggestions which may be beneficial:

The morning ritual: When we wake up, our minds are fresh and our thoughts are uncluttered. Therefore, starting the day with positive self-talk can set the tone for the rest of the day. Instead of focusing on what we need to accomplish or the challenges ahead, we should take a few minutes to acknowledge our strengths and set intentions for the day. This will help us approach the day with a positive mindset and be more resilient when faced with obstacles.

The midday slump: Midday is often the time when we hit a mental and physical slump, and negative self-talk can creep in. However, taking a break to engage in positive self-talk can help re-energize us and boost our productivity. We can use this time to affirm our strengths and remind ourselves of the progress we have made. This will help us stay motivated and focused on our goals.

The evening reflection: As the day comes to an end, it is natural to reflect on the events of the day. We should use this time to practise gratitude and self-acceptance. Reflect on our accomplishments, big or small, and acknowledge the effort we put in. Also, use this time to practise self-compassion and remind ourselves that it is okay to make mistakes and that we are doing the best we can.

The art of spending time with ourselves is a beautiful and important aspect of self-care. But how much time should we truly dedicate to it?

For some, a brief thirty-minute break from the hustle and bustle of everyday life is enough to recharge our batteries and provide the necessary clarity of mind. A few among us, however, may require a more extended period, such as an entire day or even a weekend, to truly tap into the depths of their inner world. The key is to listen to our body and mind and find a balance that works for us. Perhaps we start with fifteen minutes a day and gradually increase the time as we become more comfortable with being alone.

Regardless of the duration, what truly matters is the quality of the time spent alone. We must understand that the essence of solitude is not in the mere passing of time but in the nourishment it provides to our souls. We must learn to cherish the moments spent in our own company, for it is only when we are at peace with ourselves that we can truly connect with the world around us. Therefore, let not the clock dictate the duration of our solitude, but rather, let the experience enrich our soul and nourish our spirit.

When it comes to finding the best place for spending me-time, I recommend finding a space that allows us to get fully immersed ourselves in the present moment. This could be a cosy nook in our home, a quiet spot in Nature or even a local café that inspires creativity. Experiment with different environments until we find what works best for us.

How to take long breaks

> "Travelling—it leaves you speechless, then turns you into a storyteller."—Ibn Battuta

While taking daily breaks is essential, the value of long vacations cannot be overemphasized. Holidays offer an opportunity to unwind, relax and recharge both physically and mentally by letting us step away from our routines. Our stress reduces as we gain perspective on our lives through exploration and new experiences. Taking regular vacations promotes creativity, productivity and a balanced lifestyle. We are better able to face challenges with renewed energy and enthusiasm when we return to our daily responsibilities.

Planning a holiday can be both exciting and overwhelming. With so many options to choose from, it is important to have a strategy in place to ensure we get the most out of our vacation. Whether we are travelling solo, with friends or with family, it requires careful planning to ensure that everything goes smoothly.

Let us now explore what are some of the best strategies to follow while planning a holiday.

Determine our budget

The first step in planning a holiday is to determine our budget. It is essential to know how much money we can afford to spend on our trip. This will help us in choosing the right destination, accommodation and activities that fit our budget.

Decide on the type of holiday

Consider the kind of experience you want to have, whether it is an adventure trip, a relaxing beach holiday or a cultural exploration. This will help you narrow down your options.

Decide on the destination

The next step is to decide on the destination. We need to consider our interests and preferences, as well as the time of year we are travelling. We need to research the places we are interested in and make a list of potential destinations.

Determine the best time to travel

The time of year we travel can have a big impact on our vacation. Consider factors such as weather, crowds and pricing when choosing the best time to travel. For example, if we are planning a beach vacation, we will prefer to travel during the summer months when the weather is warm. However, this is also the peak season, so you can expect higher prices and larger crowds.

Book our accommodation

Once we have decided on our destination, it is time to book our accommodation. Consider factors such as location, price and amenities. We can book our accommodation through travel websites, directly with the hotel or through a travel agent.

Plan our activities

We must plan the activities we want to do while on a holiday. So, it is important to research the attractions, tours and experiences available at our destination. Create a rough itinerary to ensure we make the most of our time there.

Arrange transportation

Once we have planned our activities, it is time to arrange transportation. This includes flights, rental cars and local transportation. We need to make sure we book everything well in advance to avoid any last-minute surprises.

Pack appropriately

Packing is an essential part of holiday planning. Hence, we need to make a packing list, and need to include the essentials such as passports, tickets and any necessary medications. We must pack according to the climate and activities we have planned.

Purchase travel insurance

Travel insurance is essential to protect ourselves against any unforeseen circumstance such as flight cancellation, medical emergency or lost luggage. It is important to purchase travel insurance that covers all the activities we plan to do on our trip.

Stay organized

Needless to say, we should keep all our travel documents, such as our passport and boarding pass, in one place. Using a travel app or planner to keep track of our itinerary and any reservations we have made might help.

Prepare for emergencies

We must have a backup plan in case of emergencies. This includes having a contact person back home, carrying extra cash and keeping important documents in a safe place.

Enjoy ourselves

Remember, the most important part of any holiday is to enjoy ourselves! We should not stress too much about sticking to our itinerary or seeing everything on our list. It is critical to take time to relax and enjoy the moment.

Benefits of planning a holiday effectively

A holiday without proper planning can quickly turn into a stressful and disappointing experience. Whether it is a weekend getaway or a long-awaited overseas trip, effective planning is crucial to ensure a smooth and enjoyable holiday experience.

Let us explore why:

Maximizes time and resources

A good plan allows us to make the most of our time, creating a balanced itinerary that ensures we have time for relaxation and exploration. For example, if we are visiting Paris, we may want to plan our itinerary to include iconic landmarks such as the Eiffel Tower, Notre Dame Cathedral and the Louvre museum, while also leaving time to explore charming neighbourhoods, sample local cuisine and experience the Parisian culture. By planning ahead, we can avoid wasting time and money on aimless wandering or unnecessary expenses, and instead, make the most of our precious holiday time.

Helps avoid disappointments

A good plan ensures that everything we want to do and see is accounted for. We will know in advance the opening hours of the attractions we want to visit, the dress code for certain events and any cultural customs we need to be aware of. By researching the destination's weather, culture, customs and safety, we can prepare ourselves accordingly and avoid pitfalls. For instance, if we are visiting a tropical island during monsoon, we should pack rain gear and avoid booking outdoor activities that may be cancelled due to inclement weather. Likewise, if we are visiting a conservative country, we may want to dress modestly and respect local customs to avoid offending the locals or attracting unwanted attention. This knowledge can prevent us from missing out on must-see attractions and experiences or getting caught out by unexpected expenses.

Saves our hard-earned money

Effective planning helps us stick to our budget. By researching the best deals on flights, accommodation and activities, we can avoid overspending. For example, we may find a better deal on a hotel room by booking in advance or choosing to travel during the low season. Similarly, we may save money on admission fees by purchasing a city pass or booking a tour package that includes multiple attractions. By being proactive and strategic in our planning, we can stretch our budget further and have a more fulfilling holiday experience.

Encourages a sense of anticipation

The planning stage of a holiday can be just as enjoyable as the actual trip. The anticipation and excitement of researching destinations, reading reviews and choosing activities can be a thrilling experience. Having a detailed plan in place can also help us manage expectations and create a sense of anticipation that will add to the enjoyment of our holiday.

Provides peace of mind

With a good plan, we know that we have everything under control. It can be stressful to arrive at a destination without a clear plan, not knowing where to go or what to do. For example, if we are travelling to a country with a high risk of a certain disease, we can get vaccinated or take other preventive measures to protect ourselves. Similarly, if we are travelling with specific dietary restrictions, we can research the best restaurants or supermarkets to ensure that we have access to safe and healthy food options. A well-structured itinerary can alleviate this stress and provide peace of mind, allowing us to relax and enjoy our holiday.

Creates lasting memories

Finally, a well-planned itinerary ensures that we make the most of our time, creating opportunities for unforgettable experiences. Whether it is a romantic sunset on a beach, a breath-taking view from a mountaintop or a unique cultural experience, these memories will last a lifetime.

Benefits of involving our loved ones, co-travellers in travel planning

> *"Travelling in the company of those we love is home in motion."*—Leigh Hunt

Travelling is undoubtedly one of the most exhilarating experiences that we can have. The success of a trip largely depends on the planning that goes into it and it is important to involve our family, friends or co-travellers in the planning process. Why is that?

Sharing of ideas

When we involve family and friends in our holiday planning, we get to hear their ideas and preferences, which can help us to plan a more diverse and exciting itinerary. This way, everyone gets a chance to suggest places they would like to visit or activities they would prefer.

Building excitement

When everyone has a say in the planning, they are more likely to feel invested in the trip. We can discuss our plans and countdown the days until departure, which can be a fun way to get everyone excited. It also allows for open communication and the opportunity to discuss any concerns or issues that may arise.

Creating shared memories and strengthening our relationships

Travelling is all about creating memories that will last a lifetime. By involving our loved ones in the planning process, we will be creating shared memories that we will all cherish forever. From planning the itinerary to experiencing new cultures together, every step of the journey will be a bonding experience. By involving our loved ones in the planning process, we can create a trip that is not only enjoyable but also meaningful and rewarding.

Dividing responsibilities

Planning a trip can be time-consuming, and there are many tasks to complete. We can divide responsibilities among our co-travellers and share the workload. For example, one person can be responsible for booking accommodation, while another can research local attractions and activities. This approach can help reduce stress and ensure that everyone is involved in the planning process.

Accommodating everyone's preferences

Travelling with others can be challenging, especially when everyone has different preferences. By involving our loved ones in the planning process, we can accommodate everyone's preferences and create a trip that everyone will enjoy. For example, if one person prefers adventure activities while another prefers relaxing on the beach, we can plan activities that cater to both preferences.

Conclusion

In a world that seems to value constant productivity and grows increasingly hectic, it can be easy to forget the importance of taking breaks and rest. The wisdom of the Dalai Lama reminds us that cultivating inner peace and well-being is not only crucial for our own fulfilment, but also for the benefit of others.

In his teachings, the Dalai Lama emphasizes finding a balance between work and rest. According to him, true peace and happiness cannot be found solely in external circumstances or achievements. Rather, they come from cultivating a peaceful mind and a compassionate heart. And to do so, we need to take time to rest and recharge, connect with ourselves and others, and engage in activities that bring us joy and meaning.

The Dalai Lama describes mindfulness as the art of paying attention to the present moment without judgement. Mindfulness can help us become more aware of our thoughts and emotions, and develop a more compassionate and non-reactive attitude towards ourselves and others. It can also help us to appreciate the beauty and richness of life, even in its simplest moments. He also extols the value of experiencing different cultures and meeting new people, saying that travel can be a great educator and source of inspiration.

Hence, taking breaks and holidays is a powerful tool for self-betterment. By stepping away from our usual routines and obligations, we can create space to reflect on our values and priorities and return to the purpose of our lives with renewed vigour.

5 HEALTH

"Our bodies are our gardens, to which our wills are gardeners."—
William Shakespeare

In the annals of good health and what is achievable through it, there emerges a story that stands out as an example of resilience and triumph. Born in Brooklyn, New York, in 1935, Jim Morris was no stranger to the rigours of time, yet his tale would prove to be a master class in late-life renaissance.

Morris started bodybuilding in his early twenties but did not achieve much recognition in his youth. Life threw several obstacles his way, including a bout of cancer and a heart attack at age forty-five. These setbacks might have deterred many, but Morris used them as a catalyst for change. After surviving these health debacles, Morris made a conscious decision to prioritize his health. He embraced a vegan diet and began a rigorous fitness regimen. He believed that the key to good health was not only exercise, but also proper nutrition and a positive mindset.

Morris started his journey to good health at an age when many people tend to slow down. Yet, he not only regained his strength, but also surpassed his previous fitness levels. At the age of sixty-one, Morris made an astonishing comeback by winning the title of Mr Olympia Masters, an elite bodybuilding competition. He showed that even after facing significant health challenges, it is possible to not only recover but also thrive by making healthy lifestyle choices.

Morris continued to advocate for healthy diet, exercise and a holistic approach to health until his passing in 2016. His legacy is that good health is achievable through dedication, perseverance and a positive outlook on life.

Many of us go through life with the belief that the longer we live, the happier we will be. We focus on making sure we have everything we need to live a long and comfortable life. We invest in our health, accumulate wealth and plan for a retirement that we hope will last for many years. While there is nothing inherently wrong with these goals, they do not guarantee a happy and fulfilling life.

When we focus solely on extending our lives, we tend to lose sight of the things that truly matter, such as meaningful relationships, rewarding careers and the simple joys of life. We may prioritize things that ultimately do not matter in the grand scheme of things, such as material possessions or social status. In the end, we may find ourselves living a long life, but one that feels empty and incomplete. It is, therefore, imperative that we focus on living well, rather than simply living long.

Whether it is physical, mental, social or spiritual health, each aspect plays a crucial role in shaping our experiences and influencing our ability to pursue our goals and passions. Good health is a dynamic concept that involves multiple factors and influences, ranging from genetics and lifestyle to environment and social support. Achieving good health requires a holistic approach, and to that effect, we must meet certain requirements or conditions that are necessary for our well-being. Let us now explore some of the primary requirements for physical, mental, social and spiritual health and how they interact to promote overall wellness.

Factors that help maintain physical health

> "Take care of your body. It's the only place you have to live." —Jim Rohn

The human body is an intricate, complex machine that demands constant care and maintenance. When we are healthy, we are full of energy, vitality and happiness, and we can enjoy life to the fullest. On the other hand, poor health can restrict our activities, limit our potential and decrease our quality of life.

By physical health, we of course mean the optimal functioning of the body's systems and organs. It will be helpful to break down the different requirements for maintaining good physical health so that we can embrace these practices in a systematic and effective way.

Adequate nutrition

In order to maintain its physiological processes and to repair and regenerate tissue, the body needs a balanced diet, which holds pivotal importance in preserving overall physical health for various reasons. First, it provides the body with energy for physical activities. Second, it helps in maintaining proper weight and preventing obesity. Third, it helps in the prevention of chronic conditions, including heart disease, diabetes and certain types of cancer.

A balanced diet should consist of:

Carbohydrates, which are the primary source of energy for the body and can be found in foods such as rice, cereals, bread and pasta. A balanced diet should contain complex carbohydrates that are rich in fibre, such as whole grains, vegetables and fruits.

Proteins, which are essential for building and repairing tissues in the body. They are found in foods such as meat, fish, poultry, beans, lentils and nuts. A balanced diet should contain lean sources of protein, such as skinless chicken or turkey, fish, beans and lentils.

Fats, which are essential for energy, the absorption of vitamins, and the maintenance of healthy skin and hair. A balanced diet should include healthy fats, such as polyunsaturated and monounsaturated fats found in foods like nuts, seeds, oily fish and avocado. Saturated and trans fats, found in foods such as butter, cream, fatty meats and processed snacks should be limited.

Vitamins and minerals, which are found in foods such as fruits, vegetables, dairy products and lean proteins. A balanced diet should contain a variety of these foods to ensure that the body receives all the necessary nutrients.

Proper hygiene

Maintaining proper hygiene is critical for having good health because it helps prevent the spread of germs and infectious diseases. The Covid-19 pandemic highlighted the importance of hygiene, with public health officials recommending measures such as frequent hand washing, wearing masks and social distancing to prevent the spread of the virus. Good hygiene refers to the practices that help maintain cleanliness. These practices include:

Regularly washing hands with soap: By thoroughly washing our hands before meals, we remove dirt and potential contaminants, reducing the risk of ingesting harmful bacteria or viruses. After using the restroom, handwashing is crucial to eliminate any faecal matter or bacteria that may have been transferred during the process. This practice significantly reduces the risk of infections and gastrointestinal illnesses.

Taking daily showers: Daily showers or baths remove sweat, dead skin cells and dirt from the skin's surface, preventing the growth of odour-causing bacteria. It also helps in maintaining the cleanliness of hair and scalp, reducing dandruff and preventing skin issues like acne or fungal infections. How many times have we heard some snigger: "He looks unbathed"? Well, daily showers keep us looking fresh and presentable.

Brushing teeth and flossing daily: Maintaining good oral hygiene practices—a widely overlooked aspect of health—such as regular brushing and flossing are critical. Brushing removes plaque and food particles from the teeth, preventing the formation of cavities. Flossing reaches areas between teeth and along the gumline where toothbrushes cannot reach, reducing the risk of gum inflammation and bad breath.

Changing and washing clothes regularly: Regularly changing and laundering clothes are essential for maintaining personal cleanliness. Worn clothes can accumulate sweat, dead skin cells and bacteria, leading to unpleasant odours. Washing clothes helps remove stains and pathogens, ensuring that our attire remains fresh and free from potential health hazards.

Keeping living and work spaces clean: A clean living and work environment is vital for overall health. Dusting and vacuuming remove allergens and particulate matter, improving indoor air quality and reducing the risk of respiratory problems. Regular disinfection of surfaces helps prevent the spread of infectious agents, especially in shared spaces. It is particularly important during times of contagious diseases.

Regular exercise

The value of exercising regularly cannot be overestimated. Regular exercise can take multiple forms, including jogging or running in the park, attending a yoga class, lifting weights at the gym or at home, swimming, participating in a dance class, cycling through your neighbourhood, playing a game of basketball with friends, hiking in a nearby Nature trail or doing bodyweight exercises like push-ups, squats and lunges at home.

Here are some ways in which these activities can help you remain healthy:

Improve cardiovascular health: Walking, jogging and similar active exercise help improve the health of our heart and circulatory system by increasing blood flow and reducing the risk of heart disease.

Enhance lung function: Exercise helps increase lung capacity and improve oxygen uptake, which can be particularly beneficial for people with respiratory conditions.

Strengthen muscles and bones: Regular exercise helps strengthen our muscles and bones, reducing the risk of injury and falls, and improving overall mobility.

Aid in weight management: Exercise helps us burn calories and maintain a healthy weight, reducing the risk of obesity and associated health conditions.

Boost mood and mental health: Exercise and walking have been shown to improve mood and reduce symptoms of depression and anxiety by releasing endorphins, the body's natural feel-good chemicals.

Increase energy levels: Regular exercise helps increase energy levels, reduce fatigue and improve the overall quality of life.

Restful sleep

Miklós Fehér was a Hungarian footballer known for his talent on the field, having played for several clubs in Hungary and Portugal. However, on 25 January 2004, tragedy struck during a match between his team, Benfica and Vitória de Guimarães. Fehér had just been substituted into the game when he collapsed on the field. Medical staff rushed to his aid, but unfortunately, he was declared dead just a few minutes later. The cause of his death was later determined to be a heart attack, brought on by exhaustion and lack of sleep. It was discovered that Fehér had been suffering from insomnia in the weeks leading up to the match. This, coupled with the physical demands of his profession, led to his tragic death at the young age of twenty-four. Fehér's death serves as a reminder of the importance of proper rest and self-care, even for those who seem otherwise healthy and fit.

Good sleep is critical for maintaining health for several reasons. Adults need 7 to 9 hours of uninterrupted sleep each night, while children and adolescents need more. Without enough restful sleep, the body and mind cannot function at their best, leading to a range of health problems. But why is good sleep so crucial? Here are a few reasons:

Physical restoration: During sleep, the body repairs and rejuvenates itself. This is the time when the body can heal any injuries, replenish energy stores, and build and repair tissues.

Mental restoration: Sleep is also essential for mental restoration. During sleep, the brain processes the information and experiences of the day, consolidates memories and restores cognitive function. Sleep deprivation can lead to a range of mental health problems, including irritability, anxiety and depression.

Hormonal balance: Sleep also helps regulate hormones, including those that control appetite, metabolism and stress. Lack of sleep can disrupt hormone levels, leading to weight gain, metabolic disorders and increased stress levels.

Immune function: Restful sleep is critical for immune function. During sleep, the body produces cytokines, which help fight infection, inflammation and stress. Sleep deprivation can weaken the immune system and increase the risk of infections.

Avoidance of harmful substances

Philip Seymour Hoffman, a renowned American actor celebrated for his numerous cinematic and theatrical roles, battled a lifelong addiction that ultimately claimed his life. Despite accolades, including an Academy Award, Hoffman's struggle with drugs began in his early twenties and persisted despite multiple attempts at going clean. In 2013, he sought rehabilitation for heroin addiction. However in 2014, he succumbed to a drug overdose at the age of forty-six.

His untimely death shocked and saddened his admirers, highlighting the profound destructiveness of drug addiction even among successful and accomplished individuals. The aftermath witnessed an outpouring of grief and a call for enhanced support and treatment accessibility for those grappling with substance abuse. Hoffman's narrative stands as a poignant illustration of drug addiction's capacity to damage an individual's potential. It underscores the fact that individuals fighting to overcome its grip need compassionate assistance.

A few points to remember:

Avoiding harmful substances is crucial for maintaining good health due to their potential negative impacts on the body and the occurrence of various health issues. Harmful substances encompass pollutants in the air, chemicals in food, toxins in water and dangerous compounds in everyday items like cosmetics and cleaning products. Regular exposure to these substances can adversely affect organs, bodily functions and even lead to DNA damage, potentially causing cancer or chronic diseases. Smoking, alcohol, drugs and other substances can harm organs, increase chronic disease risk and contribute to premature death. Exposure to harmful substances can impact mental health, leading to conditions such as anxiety, depression and psychological issues.

By avoiding or minimizing exposure to harmful substances, we can reduce our risk of developing health problems and improve our overall well-being. This can be achieved through simple lifestyle changes like eating a healthy diet, using natural cleaning products, reducing exposure to air pollution, avoiding smoking, excessive alcohol consumption, and staying away from drugs.

Hydration

Staying properly hydrated is essential for good health, as it helps maintain normal bodily functions and prevents dehydration. Here are a few reasons why proper hydration is important:

Improved physical performance: Proper hydration improves physical performance by regulating body temperature, lubricating joints and delivering nutrients to the muscles. Dehydration can easily lead to fatigue and reduced physical performance.

Increased cognitive function: Adequate hydration fosters clear thinking. Dehydration triggers headaches and fatigue, hindering decision-making, while optimal hydration supports brain function, enhancing productivity and focus.

Better digestion: Hydration aids digestion by breaking down food and nutrient transportation. Dehydration disrupts digestion, causing issues like constipation and bloating. But when we are dehydrated, our body struggles to digest food, leading to constipation and bloating.

Improved mood: Proper hydration uplifts mood and enhances alertness, promoting positivity and productivity. Dehydration, on the other hand, causes irritability and fatigue, affecting relationships and work.

Overall health: Essential for overall health, hydration prevents conditions such as kidney stones, infections and heat stroke.

Adequate water intake safeguards against serious diseases, helping us maintain proper bodily function.

Thus, water plays a crucial role in our overall health. Despite this, we often prioritize food over proper hydration, neglecting the significance of water intake. Understanding the role of water and adequate hydration is pivotal for a healthier life.

The human body comprises approximately 60–70 per cent water, with varying percentages based on factors like age and gender. Our vital organs, including the brain, heart and lungs, heavily rely on water. From regulating body temperature and transporting nutrients to cells to detoxifying and lubricating joints, water is essential for numerous bodily functions. It contributes to healthy skin, hair, nails, brain function and energy levels.

A few points to keep in mind:

- While the recommended water intake varies by individual factors, adults generally should aim for at least eight glasses daily, spaced throughout the day.
- Carrying a reusable water bottle facilitates consistent hydration and reduces plastic waste. Additionally, certain foods like watermelon and cucumber can contribute to daily water intake.
- Water quality is equally crucial. Pollution due to industrialization and urbanization has contaminated water sources with pesticides, heavy metals and other harmful chemicals. Thus, it is important to ensure safe water consumption.
- Choosing the right type of water depends on individual preferences and needs. Alkaline water, with a higher pH, is believed to have health benefits. Bottled water is popular but can be costly and environmentally unfriendly, potentially containing high sodium levels.

- Proper water consumption practices are significant too, and we do not generally give these the necessary weight in our daily lives. These include drinking water at room temperature to avoid throat and digestive issues, sipping slowly for efficient absorption, and consuming water before and after meals for better digestion.

In short, prioritizing proper hydration is crucial for our overall well-being. A balanced approach to both the quantity and quality of water intake, along with mindful consumption habits, contributes to a healthier and more vibrant life.

Regular health check-ups

We must never neglect to keep track of our health. Let us not forget that there are many diseases and conditions that do not have discernible external symptoms. These infections or conditions can keep festering inside our bodies without our knowledge until they break out with often catastrophic consequences. Regular visits to a healthcare provider for check-ups and screenings are important for various reasons:

Prevention of diseases: Regular check-ups can help detect potential health problems before they become severe or life-threatening. Early detection of cancer, diabetes and heart disease, for instance, can significantly increase the chances of successful treatment.

Management of existing conditions: For individuals already living with a chronic illness or condition, regular check-ups can help monitor the progression of the disease and ensure that current treatments remain effective or if new treatments are required.

Mental health: Regular check-ups can also help individuals identify and manage mental health issues, such as anxiety and depression, which can affect overall health and well-being. What is more, check-ups also relieve stress or anxiety about unknown diseases or conditions.

What does good mental health look like?

"Mental health is more than the absence of mental disorders. Mental health is an integral part of health; indeed, there is no health without mental health."—World Health Organization

On 24 March 2015, Germanwings Flight 9525 flying from Barcelona to Düsseldorf tragically crashed into the French Alps, claiming the lives of all 150 individuals on board. Investigations revealed that co-pilot Andreas Lubitz deliberately caused the crash. What could have driven a young, talented pilot to commit such a heinous act? The answer lay in his deteriorating mental health. Despite a history of depression and anxiety, Lubitz hid his struggles from his employer and doctors, even tearing up a sick note that could have grounded him. This devastating event underscores the vital significance of attending to our mental well-being.

One cannot overemphasize the need for all individuals to prioritize their mental well-being, regardless of background or profession or age. By nurturing our mental health, overall quality of life, relationships and even professional performance can improve. Imagine waking up every day feeling anxious, depressed or overwhelmed. It would be difficult, if not impossible, to enjoy life's pleasures and fulfil our potential. Mental health issues such as anxiety, depression and stress can have a significant impact on our overall quality of life, affecting our relationships, work and personal life. Let us summarize what good mental health looks like:

Identifying and expressing emotions

Good mental health involves recognizing and conveying emotions effectively. Even when we are sad or frustrated, if we are able to communicate these feelings without being overwhelmed or shutting down, our mental health is good. Emotional awareness and regulation are vital for mental well-being, and can be cultivated through practices like mindfulness and cognitive-behavioural therapy. All of these practices are good at promoting healthy expression via communication, creativity or physical pursuits.

Maintaining positive relationships

Mental health also involves maintaining positive relationships with others. People who are mentally healthy tend to be good listeners, are able to empathize with others, and are generally well-liked and respected by those around them.

Managing stress effectively

Mental health includes effective stress management through activities such as exercise, meditation or simply spending time in Nature. Coping skills, such as relaxation, mindfulness and problem-solving can be used to handle stress and mental challenges successfully.

Having a sense of purpose and direction

Good mental health is also tied to having a sense of purpose and direction in life. People who are emotionally healthy tend to have a clear understanding of what they want out of life, and they work towards their goals with focus and determination.

Being resilient in the face of adversity

Individuals exhibiting mental well-being can confront challenges with resilience. Mentally healthy people can bounce back from setbacks and failures, using these experiences as opportunities for growth and learning rather than feeling overwhelmed or defeated by them.

Seeking professional help when needed

Finally, seeking help when needed is crucial, as mental health disorders can impact our quality of life and require professional treatment, such as counselling, therapy and medication. Recognizing the need for timely professional support in preserving mental well-being is itself indicative of strong mental health.

The consequences of neglecting mental health

In April 2007, tragedy struck the serene campus of Virginia Tech, a polytechnic university in Blacksburg, Virginia, USA. Seung-Hui Cho, a troubled twenty-three-year-old student with a history of mental illness, became the perpetrator of one of the deadliest school shootings in history. Despite being diagnosed with severe anxiety disorder, Cho evaded the treatment prescribed to him and spiralled deeper into darkness.

On the fateful morning of 16 April, Cho embarked on a rampage that forever scarred the Virginia Tech community. He first shot two students in a dormitory, then mailed a disturbing video manifesto to NBC News before launching a second attack at Norris Hall. Chaining doors shut to prevent escape, he unleashed chaos claiming the lives of thirty and injuring seventeen before ending his own.

The video manifesto painted a grim portrait of Cho's deteriorating mental state and his admiration for previous perpetrators of violence. The tragedy prompted a US-wide reckoning on mental healthcare, raising urgent questions about the identification and treatment of those in need.

The Virginia Tech incident reminds us of the devastating consequences of neglecting mental health. Cho's case illuminated the critical gaps in mental healthcare, a lapse that exacted a heavy toll. The story serves as a poignant reminder of the far-reaching impact of mental health challenges. Beyond personal suffering, untreated mental health issues can lead to catastrophic outcomes affecting not only the afflicted individual but also entire communities.

Mental health disorders can be incredibly debilitating, and they can affect all aspects of our lives, from our relationships and work to our physical health and sense of self. It is important to identify such problems so that we can help ourselves and others around us. Let us look at some of the common mental health disorders and understand how they affect our daily lives:

Depression

Depression is a common mental disorder causing sadness, hopelessness, loss of interest, sleep issues and fatigue. It affects our capacity to focus, take decisions, do tasks and maintain relationships.

Anxiety

Anxiety causes restlessness, panic and palpitations. It hinders stress management, social engagement and the quality of life.

Psychotic disorder

Psychosis causes delusions, hallucinations and disorganized thinking, impeding communication and daily tasks.

Substance-use disorder

These are addictions caused by an inability to cope with mental health issues. Addiction to drugs and other harmful substances can lead to legal, relational and physical issues.

Personality disorders

These include borderline and narcissistic personality disorders. While the former is marked by an inability to regulate emotions, the latter manifests in a lack of empathy. These disorders alter perception, social interactions as well as personal and professional relationships.

Bipolar disorder

This disorder is marked by mood swings from highs (called mania) to lows (called depression). One experiences emotions such as euphoria, irritability, disrupted energy, sleep and impulsivity, lasting days or weeks.

Schizophrenia

This is a serious disorder affecting thinking, emotions and behaviour. Symptoms include delusions, hallucinations, disorganized thinking and loss of motivation.

In addition to all these, poor mental health can also contribute to other mental health disorders such as obsessive-compulsive disorder (OCD), post-traumatic stress disorder (PTSD) and eating disorders. It is important to note that mental health disorders can affect anyone, regardless of age, gender, race or socioeconomic status. Seeking help from a mental health professional can be beneficial in managing mental health disorders and promoting overall mental health and well-being.

Why mental health is still a taboo in our society?

> "Mental illness is nothing to be ashamed of,
> but stigma and bias shame us all."—Bill Clinton

Mental health is a topic that is often shrouded in secrecy, and discussing it openly is frowned upon in many parts of the world. Despite the significant strides in medical research, modern technology and access to information, society still considers mental health to be a taboo topic. Many people still feel uncomfortable discussing their own mental health issues or that of their loved ones.

The stigma surrounding mental illness is not only detrimental to those who are struggling, but also to society as a whole. It creates a culture of fear, shame and isolation, which makes it harder for individuals to seek help or support, leading to delayed treatment and even suicide. Moreover, it affects the productivity and economic growth of a society, as individuals who are struggling with mental illness are less likely to be able to contribute fully to the workforce.

The complexity of mental health is closely linked to history, culture and social norms. Many societies, often rife with misconceptions, label mental illness as weakness or divine punishment. The media, too, has played its part by perpetuating stereotypes and portraying those with mental health issues as dangerous or unproductive. There is even a persistent belief that mental health is solely a result of personal choices, dismissing genetic and environmental or conditional factors. This misunderstanding leads to blame and judgement towards those struggling with their mental health. Furthermore, unlike many physical challenges, mental health struggles are often hidden and invisible, leading to scepticism about their seriousness. In addition, mental health services are often inaccessible or unaffordable. The lack of funding and resources for mental health research and services perpetuates the notion that mental health is not a priority.

To dismantle this stigma, raising awareness is crucial. Acknowledging mental health as a legitimate medical concern is essential, supported by proper media representation and campaigns. Recognizing signs, offering support and debunking myths are the vital steps. Overall, cultivating a compassionate culture that fosters acceptance and empathy is imperative. Facilitating open conversations, free from prejudice and discrimination, allows individuals to share their experiences without fear. Breaking the taboo around mental health requires collective efforts to foster understanding, acceptance and support.

Understanding the main causes behind rising mental health issues

Mental health issues have become increasingly prevalent and a growing concern worldwide in recent times. The World Health Organization (WHO) in a June 2022 report estimates that one in eight people globally are living with mental disorders, which amounts to at least 970 million people. And alarmingly enough, these numbers are rising. So, what are the main reasons for this? While there may be several factors contributing to the rise in mental health problems, here we may aim to explore some of the most significant ones:

Rise of social media

The rise of social media has led to heightened isolation and detachment from reality. Many people, especially youth, spend hours scrolling through their social media feeds, comparing themselves to others and feeling inadequate. This fosters unrealistic standards, resulting in diminished self-esteem, depression and anxiety. Constant technological engagement hampers relaxation, disrupts sleep and elevates stress.

Increased stress

The current age has brought with it increased stress and pressure. Many people are juggling multiple responsibilities, such as work, family and social obligations, which can take a toll on their mental health. With the rise of the gig economy and the prevalence of insecure work, many are working multiple jobs and longer hours. This inability to switch off from work can lead to burnout and anxiety. The pressure to meet deadlines, handle workloads and achieve targets can cause significant stress and negatively impact mental health.

Trauma and abuse

Trauma and abuse, including childhood abuse, domestic violence and sexual assault, can lead to enduring mental health problems like PTSD, depression and anxiety. Such experiences, including accidents, violence and natural disasters, leave emotional wounds, potentially triggering lasting mental health conditions.

Environmental factors

Research has revealed the profound impact of environmental factors on mental health. Air and noise pollution, availability of green spaces, natural disasters and climate change are influential factors. Pollution can impair cognition, with air pollution linked to anxiety, depression and suicide risk. Noise pollution induces stress, sleep disruption and cognitive impairment. Conversely, access to Nature helps alleviate depression and anxiety. Natural disasters like hurricanes and earthquakes yield long-term mental health consequences, including PTSD, depression and anxiety.

Climate anxiety

A condition that is being increasingly noticed nowadays by psychologists is climate anxiety—a state of great unease concerning climate change and its ramifications for the environment and human life. This can manifest as intrusive thoughts or feelings of apprehension regarding potential catastrophes, the enduring prospects of humanity and the planet as well as the well-being of the future generations. It encompasses physiological aspects, such as an increased heart rate and breathlessness along with behavioural elements. These include instances where climate anxiety impedes an individual's ability to maintain healthy social relationships or perform effectively in their professional or educational endeavours.

Lack of support

Despite increased awareness about mental health issues, there is still a significant stigma attached to seeking help. Many people feel embarrassed or ashamed to talk about their mental struggles and tend to suffer in silence. Additionally, there is not enough support and resources for those who do seek help, which perpetuates mental health problems.

Genetics and biology

Mental health issues can also be influenced by genetics and biology. For example, some people may be more susceptible to conditions such as depression or bipolar disorder due to their genes. Chemical imbalances in the brain, such as a lack of serotonin or dopamine, can contribute to depression or anxiety. Additionally, structural differences in the brain, such as those found in people with autism or attention-deficit/hyperactivity disorder, can also contribute to mental health issues.

Reasons behind increasing mental health issues among children

Childhood is typically associated with carefree joy and boundless energy. But today it is witnessing an unsettling rise in mental health issues among children. The WHO reports that one in eight people globally is affected by mental health disorders, with half of these conditions emerging by the age fourteen. This trend is reflected in the US, where the Centers for Disease Control and Prevention (CDC) found that 17.4 per cent of American children aged 2–8 years have diagnosed mental, behavioural or developmental disorders, including anxiety, depression and attention deficit hyperactivity disorder (ADHD). The surge in these challenges can be attributed to several factors.

First, mounting academic and social pressures are placing considerable strain on children. Educational systems have grown fiercely competitive, urging students to excel academically and in extracurricular activities. This pressure can be overwhelming, leading to stress, anxiety and even depression. This is particularly observed among young adults aged 18–25, with 33.7 per cent experiencing mental illness, according to the National Institute of Mental Health (NIMH).

Moreover, the omnipresence of technology is making the situation worse. Prolonged screen exposure and social media use contribute to sedentary behaviour, anxiety, depression and feelings of inadequacy due to unfavourable comparisons with peers. Additionally, cyberbullying on these platforms is detrimental: 59 per cent of US teens have encountered abusive online behaviour, as per a 2018 Pew Research Center survey.

The evolving family landscape—with increasing divorce rates and single-parent households—adds to children's emotional struggles. Such changes can breed insecurity and instability, affecting mental health. Studies indicate that children from single-parent households are more vulnerable to mental health issues.

The Covid-19 pandemic has adversely impacted children's mental health too, with disrupted routines, social isolation, and fear causing a surge in anxiety and depression. According to a study published in the renowned journal *Lancet* in October 2021, two Covid-19 impact indicators, specifically daily SARS-CoV-2 infection rates and reductions in human mobility, were linked to increased prevalence of major depressive disorder.

Trauma also contributes to the rise of mental health issues in children. The long-term repercussions of trauma—whether physical or emotional—can lead to anxiety, depression and other disorders. According to the Substance Abuse and Mental Health Services Administration (SAMHSA) in the US, more than two-thirds of children reported at least one traumatic event by age sixteen.

Steps to address mental health issues in loved ones

Support from family members and partners plays a pivotal role in managing and recovering from mental health issues. Understanding the condition and its symptoms is crucial. Creating a support system, listening, offering reassurance and creating a safe environment are vital. Given the stigma associated with mental health, loved ones' understanding and empathy are indispensable.

Therefore, supporting a loved one with mental illness can be a challenging and daunting task. Here are some strategies that family members and partners can consider for providing effective support:

Educate ourselves

Understanding the signs and symptoms of mental illness can help family members and partners provide more effective support. Educating ourselves about mental illness can also help us better advocate for our loved ones' needs.

Communicate openly

Communication is key when supporting a loved one with a mental illness. We need to be open and honest about our feelings and concerns and encourage our loved ones to do the same. Avoid judging or criticizing and focus on offering support and understanding.

Offer emotional support

Mental illness can be isolating and overwhelming for those experiencing it. Family members and partners can provide emotional support by listening to their loved ones' concerns, offering reassurance and being there for them during difficult times. It is also important not to invalidate or dismiss their feelings.

Provide practical support

Mental illness can make even the simplest of tasks seem overwhelming. Family members and partners can provide practical support by helping with household tasks, providing transportation to appointments or assisting with medication management.

Encourage treatment

Encouraging our loved one to seek treatment is crucial. This can involve helping them find a therapist, accompanying them to appointments or providing financial support if needed. One must remember that seeking treatment is a brave and important step towards recovery.

Foster healthy habits

Healthy habits such as regular exercise, a proper diet and getting enough sleep also help combat mental health issues. A partner or family member can offer support in developing and maintaining these habits.

Encourage hobbies and interests

Engaging in hobbies or activities we love can lead us away from negative thoughts and provide a sense of purpose. A partner or family member can offer support by engaging in these activities with their loved ones and encouraging them to pursue their interests.

Be patient and understanding

Dealing with the mental health issues of partners and loved ones can be a long and difficult journey. It is important to be patient, understanding and non-judgmental.

Seek support for ourselves

Supporting a loved one with a mental illness can be emotionally and physically draining. It is essential to take care of our own needs as well. Consider joining a support group or seeking counselling.

The inspiring mental health journey of Lady Gaga: Who does not know Lady Gaga? The renowned pop icon has captivated the world with her distinctive music and style. But amid her accolades, including thirteen Grammys and over forty million albums sold globally, lies a lesser-known struggle with mental health issues. Gaga, whose original name is Stefani Joanne Angelina Germanotta, confronted depression, anxiety and panic attacks from a young age. But she sought professional help to navigate these challenges. In 2017, she disclosed her battle with PTSD, revealing her past sexual assault at nineteen and the resultant depression and anxiety.

In 2018, Gaga's journey was further complicated by fibromyalgia-induced severe pain, prompting her to cancel tour dates. At her lowest point, she grappled with suicidal thoughts. Throughout her struggles, her partner Christian Carino, a talent agent, played a pivotal role. He supported her through the darkest moments and encouraged professional help. With Carino's unstinting backing, Gaga embraced therapy, meditation, yoga and holistic practices like Reiki and sound baths to foster recovery.

In 2019, Gaga's role in the movie *A Star Is Born*, addressing mental health and addiction, earned her an Oscar. This portrayal resonated globally and underscored the significance of mental health. Lady Gaga now uses her platform to champion mental health awareness, emphasizing the importance of seeking assistance in times of struggle. Her story shows that mental health issues can affect anyone, irrespective of fame, but that with proper support and treatment, individuals can overcome them and attain remarkable achievements.

What does good social health look like?

> "A healthy social life is found only when, in the mirror of each soul, the whole community finds its reflection, and when, in the whole community, the virtue of each one is living." —Rudolf Steiner

The third pillar of health is social health. A person who is socially healthy has meaningful relationships with family, friends and community. They feel a sense of belonging in society and when they are in need, society rallies to support them. Good physical and mental health is essential for our social health because when we are physically and mentally fit, we can attend social gatherings, participate in hobbies and engage in community activities. A healthy individual can travel the world, experience new cultures and meet new people; an unhealthy person may not be able to do so, leading to social isolation and loneliness, which can have a negative impact on their mental health.

Consider a young woman with a cancer diagnosis challenging her physical health and emotions. With proper help like therapy, support groups and loved ones, she can ensure mental and social well-being, enhancing her recovery prospects. Similarly, an elderly retired man can sustain his mental and social health through hobbies, volunteering, and meaningful friendships and relationships. Prioritizing social health enables us to maintain purpose, connections and fulfilment despite life's turbulent changes, so it is important to recognize what good social health looks like. Here are some signs:

Ability to establish positive relationships

People who are socially healthy can build positive relationships with others. This might involve making new friends, deepening existing friendships or building strong relationships with family members or romantic partners.

Conduct effective communication

Social health also means being able to communicate effectively with others. This implies being able to express our needs and feelings clearly.

Ability to empathize

The ability to understand and empathize with others is a bedrock of building social health. Empathy can be practised through active listening.

Feeling supported

When we see that our kith and kin are available to provide emotional support during times of stress or difficulty, we know that we are leading a socially healthy life.

Being an active contributor to society

Social health also involves contributing to the community in a positive way. This might mean volunteering, participating in community events or simply being a good neighbour and building a sense of community in our local area.

Being culturally aware

Understanding and respecting different cultures is an essential sign of good social health. This includes a curiosity about and an appreciation for diversity and promoting social justice.

Having a sense of belonging

People who are socially healthy tend to feel connected with their community, and they have a sense of purpose and meaning that comes from their relationships with others. They also tend to be happier and more fulfilled than those who feel isolated or disconnected from others.

Making the best of social networks

> "Surround yourself with those who only lift you higher."—Oprah Winfrey

As social creatures, humans are wired to seek out connections with others. We form friendships, romantic partnerships and professional networks that shape our daily lives. But beyond the immediate gratification of social interactions, the people we associate with can have long-lasting effects on our personal and professional development.

It is often said that we are the average of the five people we spend the most time with. This is a powerful statement that holds a lot of truth. The company we keep can have a profound impact on the trajectory of our life. Think about it. Our friends, family and colleagues reflect who we are, what we value and the direction in which we are headed. They can either uplift us, inspire us and encourage us to achieve our goals or bring us down, hinder our progress and derail our dreams. Their attitudes, beliefs and habits can rub off on us, shaping our worldview and shaping our future. As the saying goes, "Birds of a feather flock together". In fact, research has shown that the people we surround ourselves with can significantly influence our behaviour, beliefs and ultimately, our success.

The influence of our social network can be particularly potent during key transitional periods in our lives, such as adolescence, early adulthood and career transitions. During these times, we are more susceptible to the opinions, attitudes and behaviours of those around us. In some cases, this can be positive, leading us to make better decisions, take risks and pursue our goals with greater vigour. But in other cases, it can be negative, leading us down a path of self-destruction, missed opportunities and unfulfilled potential.

One of the primary ways in which our social network shapes us is through the transmission of ideas and values. We absorb the beliefs and opinions of those around us, and over time, they become integrated into our own worldview. This is particularly true when it comes to moral and ethical values, which are often learned through socialization processes that occur in childhood and early adolescence. If we are surrounded by people who have a strong sense of integrity, honesty and compassion, we are more likely to adopt these values as our own. Conversely, if we associate with people who have a more cynical, self-centred or unethical outlook on life, we may find ourselves becoming the same.

The people we associate with can also have a profound impact on our behaviour. Studies have shown that we are more likely to engage in certain activities if we see our peers doing them. If we spend time with people who engage in healthy habits such as exercising, eating well and getting enough rest, we are more likely to adopt these habits as well. In contrast, if we constantly hang out with people who engage in unhealthy habits such as smoking, drinking and excessive partying, we may pick up these vices too. Therefore, it is important to surround ourselves with people who have healthy habits and behaviours that align with our goals.

Our social networks can also influence our opportunities and access to resources. If we associate with people who are successful, well connected and supportive, we are more likely to have access to opportunities that can advance our careers or personal goals.

On the other hand, if the people around us are negative, unsupportive, or have limited resources, we may find ourselves stagnating, with few opportunities for growth or advancement. The more varied and inclusive our network, the more access we have to different perspectives, resources, and experiences which can broaden our horizons and help us to grow. Diversity is crucial for personal growth, and we can learn a lot from people with different backgrounds, experiences and viewpoints. However, we must be mindful of the kind of company we keep. We should seek out people who challenge us to be our best selves, support us in our endeavours, and share our values and principles.

Lastly, the people we surround ourselves with can have a significant impact on our emotional well-being. If we spend time with people who are positive, supportive and uplifting, we are more likely to feel happy and fulfilled. Spending time with negative, critical and unsupportive people has the exact opposite effect. Positive people generally have a can-do attitude and are driven to achieve their goals. When we surround ourselves with such people, we can be inspired to be our best selves and pursue our dreams with greater determination.

What does good spiritual health look like?

> "You have to grow from the inside out. None can teach you, none can make you spiritual. There is no other teacher but your own soul."—Swami Vivekananda

Spiritual health is a state of being where an individual feels connected to something greater than themselves, whether it is the natural world, a higher power, or their inner self. Spiritual health is not just about religion, it is a broader concept that encompasses all aspects of human experience, including personal values, beliefs and emotions. When we have a strong spiritual connection, we feel grounded, fulfilled and content. Let me share a summary of what I believe good spiritual health looks like:

Having a sense of purpose

At the core of spiritual health is a profound sense of purpose, something we discussed at length in the Introduction. This involves finding fulfilment in meaningful experiences and going far beyond the pursuit of material gains or external accomplishments. To achieve this, we must identify our personal values, set goals and cultivate beliefs that resonate with our core being. Having a sense of purpose adds depth and richness to our lives.

Maintaining inner peace

Inner peace represents a state of mental calm and contentment, and is a hallmark of spiritual health. This is a form of emotional resilience which allows us to maintain stability even in the face of challenges. A sense of inner peace fosters a serene outlook on life, reducing stress and promoting overall well-being.

Capacity to forgive

Ability to forgive, be compassionate and empathize, play a pivotal role in our spiritual health. These qualities strengthen bonds in our relationships and promote understanding and goodwill. If we are able to forgive others—and ourselves—for the wrongs committed in the past, we will gain a sense of emotional liberation. It will enable us to release the burden of grudges, after which we can move forward with an open heart.

Ability to self-reflect

Taking time out for introspection and meditation allows us to explore our inner landscape. It encourages growth through questioning and analysing beliefs and values. Self-reflection fosters personal development, leading to a deeper understanding of ourselves and our place in the world.

Commitment to personal growth

Spiritual health is reflected in a commitment to inner growth. This commitment involves nurturing qualities that we are discussing throughout this book: from honesty to humility and humaneness. By continually working on personal growth, we become better versions of ourselves and contribute positively to the world around us.

Having a sense of belonging

In the end, belonging to a like-minded community is an important facet of spiritual health. Being part of a community that shares similar beliefs and values offers support and validation. This can be a community of hobbyists, holidaymakers, social-work volunteers or a group that shares our religious faith. Belonging reinforces a sense of identity and provides a space for us to connect with others who understand and respect our life's journey. It can be a source of comfort and strength.

These elements work together and nurture the soul and promote the overall well-being thus creating a rich and fulfilling life.

Conclusion

Blue Zones are unique regions scattered across the world where a remarkable number of people live past 100 years while maintaining exceptional well-being. The term "Blue Zone" was coined by journalist Dan Buettner, who identified these areas as sharing certain characteristics that contribute to people's longevity.

For instance, Blue Zones like Okinawa, Japan, emphasize a plant-based diet, regular exercise and strong social connections. The people there practise *hara hachi bu*, a tradition of eating until one is 80 per cent full. Sardinia, Italy, on the other hand, boasts a Mediterranean diet rich in whole grains, vegetables, fruits and healthy fats, along with an active lifestyle and close social ties. Costa Rica's Nicoya region follows a traditional lifestyle centred on family, faith and farming, with a plant-based diet and strong community support. The Greek island of Ikaria emphasizes simplicity, stress-free living and a Mediterranean diet rich in olive oil, vegetables and whole grains. All these regions have low instances of chronic diseases and high life expectancies.

The term "Blue Zone" possibly refers to the blue circles drawn on a map to denote these regions or the serene environment they offer. These areas hold valuable lessons for healthy living, including balanced diets, physical activity, social engagement and purpose-driven lives. The lifestyles of these long-lived communities emphasize community involvement, mindfulness and the appreciation of life's simple joys.

We have the power to cultivate our own Blue Zones by prioritizing our well-being across physical, mental, social and spiritual dimensions. Through the right habits and practices discussed in this chapter, we too can prove that age-defying health and happiness can be achieved by adopting a holistic approach to well-being.

6 HUMILITY

HUMILITY

> "Humility is the mother of giants. One sees great things from the valley; only small things from the peak." —G. K. Chesterton

There once was a man named Abdul Sattar Edhi. He was born in the city of Bantwa in Gujarat, India, in 1928, and emigrated to Pakistan during the Partition of India. He began his life's work in Karachi, one of the most populous and poverty-stricken cities in the country. Starting his journey with just a few rupees in his pocket, and a dream to serve humanity, he went on to establish the Edhi Foundation in 1951, which provided free healthcare, food and shelter to the needy, regardless of their religion or ethnicity.

Edhi would personally drive the ambulances, pick up bodies of the deceased, and care for the sick and dying. Edhi never forgot his roots and remained humble throughout his life. He lived in a small room in the foundation's office, sleeping on a bed that was nothing more than a thin mat on the floor. Even though his foundation went on to run the world's largest volunteer ambulance network, Edhi never allowed his success to get to his head. He would often be seen walking the streets of Karachi, dressed in simple clothes, collecting donations in a small metal box. He would wash the feet of the homeless, clean their wounds, and provide them with food and shelter. He never sought recognition or praise for his work, often telling journalists that he was just doing what he felt was his duty as a human being.

Edhi's work had a profound impact on the lives of countless individuals in Pakistan. His selfless service to humanity soon gained recognition, and he received numerous awards and accolades for his work, including the Ramon Magsaysay Award, often referred to as the "Asian Nobel Prize", in 1986 and the Seoul Peace Prize in 2008. More importantly, his humility and dedication inspired countless others to follow in his footsteps. He showed that true greatness lies not in wealth or power, but in service to others.

Abdul Sattar Edhi's life is a testament to the power of humility. He showed that by putting others before ourselves, we can create a world that is full of love, compassion and kindness.

The importance of humility: a look at the religions of the world

Throughout history, various religions have emerged, each with its unique set of teachings and principles. One value that is consistently emphasized across different faiths is the importance of humility, that is, the quality of being humble and modest. The word "humility" derives from the Latin *humilitas*, which means "grounded" or "low". It is the opposite of arrogance, self-centredness and pride.

Humility is seen as a fundamental virtue that helps individuals connect with the divine. By recognizing one's own limitations and faults, a person can cultivate a sense of reverence for the sacred. Humility also allows individuals to see the interconnectedness of all things, to recognize the inherent dignity and worth of every person, and to act with compassion and empathy towards others.

Let us look at some examples.

Christianity

Jesus Christ himself demonstrated the virtue of humility by washing his disciples' feet, a task usually reserved for servants. Christians are urged to "Do nothing out of selfish ambition or vain conceit. Rather, in humility value others above yourselves" (Philippians 2:3, New International Version) and to "clothe yourselves with humility toward one another because God opposes the proud but gives grace to the humble" (1 Peter 5:5, NIV). According to the teachings of Christianity, "Those who exalt themselves will be humbled, and those who humble themselves will be exalted" (Matthew 23:12, NIV).

Islam

Muslims are urged to recognize their own insignificance in the grand scheme of things and to submit to God's will. Humility is linked to the concept of *tawhid* or the oneness of God. Prophet Muhammad said, "He who has in his heart the weight of a mustard seed of pride shall not enter Paradise" (Sahih Muslim 91c). One of the five pillars of Islam is *zakat*, which requires Muslims to give a portion of their wealth to those in need. Muslims are also encouraged to perform acts of service, such as volunteering in their community. As the Prophet said, "The best of people are those who are most beneficial to others" (al-Mu'jam al-Awsat, 5937).

Buddhism

The Buddhist concept of *metta* or loving-kindness emphasizes compassion and service towards others. Buddha himself said that "the fragrance of flowers and of good deeds travels with the wind" and that "the fragrance of sandalwood or of rosebay does not travel far" (Dhammapada 2). This implies that one should not boast of their good deeds but instead remain humble and modest. By cultivating humility, Buddhists believe one can break free from the cycle of suffering, detach oneself from the ego and attain a state of inner peace, thereby achieving enlightenment.

Sikhism

The Guru Granth Sahib teaches that humility is the foundation of all virtues and that it is the key to achieving a connection with the divine. In Sikhism, humility is expressed through the concept of *seva* or selfless service, without any expectation of reward or recognition. According to Sikh teachings, the ego is the root of all suffering and separation from God, and humility is the antidote to this spiritual ailment. One who calls himself "a lowly servant of God, and thinks himself as such, shall attain honour in the Court of the Lord" (Sri Guru Granth Sahib, Ang 1133). This verse emphasizes the idea that true humility involves surrendering our will to the divine, recognizing that we are all part of a greater whole.

Taoism

The *Tao Te Ching* states, "The highest goodness is like water. Water knows how to benefit all things without striving with them. It rests at the lowest place, a place where no one wishes to stay" (Chapter 8). According to Lao Tzu, a wise person does not hold on to material possessions but instead focuses on helping others. By doing so, the person also gains benefits. They follow this path by taking action without engaging in unnecessary competition. Ultimately, the message is about the virtue of giving, the harmony of the natural order and the wisdom in non-competitive actions.

The path of humility in Hinduism

Hinduism is a vast and intricate faith that promotes the unity of all living beings and recognizes the divine essence in all things. In the Hindu worldview, humility is not just a virtue but a way of life that leads to self-realization and liberation from the cycle of birth and death. At the core of Hinduism lies the belief in the interconnectedness of all beings and recognizing that we are but a small part of a greater cosmic whole. This realization helps to acknowledge that no one is superior or inferior to another.

The Hindu scriptures are replete with stories and teachings that illustrate the beauty of humility. For example, the Bhagavad Gita states, "He who regards all beings as equal, whether in pleasure or in pain, is a yogi of the highest order" (Chapter 6, Verse 32). One of the most significant ways in which Hinduism promotes humility is through the concept of karma, the law of cause and effect that governs the universe. The Gita teaches that we should perform our duties without being attached to the results of our actions. By focusing on the process rather than the result, we develop a sense of detachment and humility, recognizing that we are not in control of the outcome.

Furthermore, Hinduism teaches that humility is necessary for the pursuit of knowledge. The seeker of knowledge must approach the teacher with a humble attitude, recognizing that they have much to learn and that the teacher is a guide on their journey. This attitude of humility allows the seeker to absorb knowledge with an open mind.

Like Sikhism, Hinduism also promotes humility through *seva*. By serving others, we develop a deep sense of empathy and compassion, which leads to humility. Humility is essential in one's relationship with God, as the devotee must recognize their own limitations and surrender to the divine will. This surrender is not an act of defeat but a recognition that the divine is the ultimate source of power and wisdom. In the words of the Gita, "Abandon all varieties of religion and just surrender unto me. I shall deliver you from all sinful reactions. Do not fear" (Chapter 18, Verse 66).

The multifaceted nature of humility

There are various types of humility. Let us explore some of them and examine how they can enrich our lives and relationships.

Intellectual humility

Let us say you are someone who strongly believes in a particular political ideology. However, you come across an article that presents an argument against your ideology that you have not considered before. Rather than dismiss it, you take the time to read the article, consider its points and even do some additional research. After careful consideration, you realize that some of the arguments presented in it are valid, and you begin to question some of your previously held beliefs.

This is intellectual humility, which involves being open to alternative viewpoints, acknowledging the possibility of incomplete or flawed knowledge, and remaining receptive to new information and ideas. This approach leads to a more nuanced understanding of and appreciation for the complexity and diversity of the world. Embracing intellectual humility fosters deeper insights and a willingness to evolve our perspective through continuous learning and consideration of diverse viewpoints.

Moral humility

Moral humility allows us to acknowledge our own imperfections and shortcomings, and to recognize the humanity in others, even when they may have done wrong. It requires us to recognize that there are different cultural and religious beliefs and practices which are all valid. For example, someone who grew up in a culture that practices arranged marriages may have a different perspective on love and marriage from someone who grew up in a culture that emphasizes individual choice and autonomy.

Moral humility involves acknowledging that our personal experiences and biases may limit our understanding of issues. A person who has never experienced poverty, for instance, may struggle to understand the challenges faced by poor people and may need to listen to their perspectives to gain a fuller understanding.

Moral humility also requires being open to feedback and criticism from others, and engaging in self-reflection and self-criticism. When we embrace moral humility, we become less judgmental and more compassionate, forgiving and understanding, acknowledging that everyone is navigating life's complexities in their own way.

Social humility

Social humility allows us to acknowledge the ways in which our social identities—such as race, gender, class or sexuality—may have given us advantages or disadvantages in life. It involves valuing and respecting the diversity of people and cultures around us, and seeking out opportunities to learn from them.

Social humility requires actively listening to people from different backgrounds, without assumptions or judgements.

By recognizing our own biases, we can cultivate empathy and understand others' experiences. Just like moral humility, we need to be open to feedback if we are to practise social humility. This helps us learn and become better advocates for diversity and inclusion.

Embracing social humility leads to a more just and equitable society by fostering genuine understanding, reducing harmful stereotypes and supporting marginalized communities through meaningful action.

The value of humility

In a world that often glorifies individual achievement and self-promotion, the virtue of humility can seem like a relic from a bygone era. Yet, far from being a sign of weakness or being old-fashioned, humility is a powerful and transformative force. Of course, cultivating humility is not easy as it requires a willingness to let go of our ego. Yet, the rewards of cultivating this virtue are profound and long-lasting. Let us look at some of the key benefits of humility as a virtue:

Builds stronger relationships

When we are humble, we are more likely to listen to others, seek out their perspectives and take their needs into account. Thus, humility fosters empathy and understanding towards others.

Promotes personal growth

Humility also makes us open to learning and growth. We are willing to admit when we do not know something and seek out new knowledge and experiences.

Enhances leadership

When leaders are humble, they are more likely to listen to and understand the needs of their team members. They are also more likely to admit when they are wrong and make course corrections as needed. Both these make leaders more effective and successful.

Fosters gratitude

Humility fosters gratitude, enabling us to appreciate the beauty and worth of others and ourselves. It encourages us to cherish the richness of our present experience and acknowledge the contributions of others to our achievements, cultivating a deeper appreciation for the world around us.

Nurtures genuineness and authenticity

Humility enhances authenticity and attracts others. Embracing vulnerability and admitting shortcomings fosters trust and intimacy in relationships, especially in romantic ones, where honesty and vulnerability are vital for meaningful connections.

Leads to inner peace

Humility brings inner peace and contentment independent of external factors. Being less attached to others' opinions or the need for validation reduces anxiety and stress, fostering joy in being present and engaged in the moment.

Tips and techniques of expressing humility

> "Humility is not thinking less of yourself, it's thinking of yourself less."—C. S. Lewis

How can we express humility and make it a part of our daily existence? Here are some of the best ways to do so:

By listening actively

When we listen to others, we show them respect and value their opinions. Active listening involves paying attention to what others are saying without interrupting or judging them. It also involves asking questions to clarify any misunderstandings and showing empathy and understanding.

By admitting our mistakes

No one is perfect; everyone makes mistakes. Acknowledging our mistakes and taking responsibility for them shows that we are willing to learn and grow. It also helps to build trust and credibility with others.

By showing gratitude

Being grateful for what we have and the people in our lives helps us to stay humble. When we focus on the good things in our lives, we are less likely to become complacent or take things for granted. Gratitude also helps us appreciate the efforts of others and the contributions they make to our lives.

By seeking feedback

Asking for feedback from others can be a humbling experience. It requires us to be open to criticism and to be willing to make changes based on that feedback. Seeking feedback also shows that we value the opinions of others and are willing to learn from them.

By serving others

When we put the needs of others before our own, we demonstrate that we are not self-centred or egotistical. Serving others also helps us to develop empathy and compassion, which are essential qualities for humility.

By being open-minded

Having an open mind means being willing to consider new ideas and perspectives. It requires us to be flexible and adaptable and to recognize that we do not have all the answers.

By avoiding self-promotion

Humble individuals do not seek attention or recognition for their accomplishments and instead focus on the needs and interests of others.

Humility vs arrogance: the battle within

No discussion on humility can be complete without the exploration of its opposite: arrogance. Pride is a natural human emotion that comes from a sense of accomplishment, confidence and self-respect. However, when it becomes excessive, it can lead to arrogance, which leads to an exaggerated sense of self, a lack of consideration for others and a tendency to put oneself first.

Arrogance can manifest in various forms, ranging from subtle displays of superiority to overt displays of dominance. It will be helpful here to explore humility and pride using examples to illustrate the nuances of these two opposing qualities.

For instance, a humble leader listens to their team's input and considers everyone's ideas before deciding; an arrogant leader makes decisions based solely on their own beliefs. A humble student asks questions and seeks knowledge from their teachers and peers; an arrogant student thinks they know everything and dismisses the knowledge of others.

A humble person is quick to acknowledge their own limitations. If they are struggling with a particular task, they will be willing to ask for help and guidance from an expert. On the other hand, a proud person is unwilling to admit their drawbacks and tend to belittle others. While a humble person treats others with respect and kindness, regardless of their status, wealth or background, a proud person, in contrast, sees others as inferior and not worth listening to.

We are humble when we approach life with a sense of gratitude and appreciation for what we have, recognizing that our achievements are not solely a result of our own efforts but also the contributions of others and circumstances outside our control. A proud person, on the other hand, tends to take full credit for whatever they have achieved.

It is not hard to trace the roots of arrogance back to our achievements or successes. When we accomplish something significant, it is natural to feel proud. However, pride in achievements can easily lead to arrogance and entitlement if unchecked. Arrogance results in a loss of respect from others, leading to negative consequences such as losing friends, business deals or even jobs. Thinking too much of ourselves, being overconfident in our abilities and refusing to listen to others' opinions can lead to poor decision-making and further negative outcomes.

History is replete with figures whose downfall can be attributed to this hubris. Julius Caesar, Emperor Nero, King Louis XVI, Napoleon Bonaparte, Emperor Hirohito, Idi Amin, Saddam Hussein and Muammar Gaddafi all played significant roles in history. But they also shared a common trait of arrogance and overconfidence. This caused them to make poor decisions, ignore dissenting voices and ultimately lose power through assassination, execution, overthrow or defeat in battles. Their stories serve as cautionary examples of the consequences of unchecked pride and the importance of humility in leadership.

The power of healthy pride

Pride is a complex emotion that can have both positive and negative effects on our lives. While excessive pride can lead to arrogance, self-centredness and a lack of empathy for others, a healthy sense of pride, on the other hand, can boost our self-esteem and motivate us to achieve our goals. In experiencing healthy pride, we feel peace, contentment and confidence.

Having a healthy sense of pride can have many positive effects on our life, such as:

Increased self-esteem

When we take pride in our accomplishments, whether big or small, it bolsters our self-worth. This boost in self-esteem becomes a valuable asset as it gives us the confidence needed to tackle new challenges and surmount obstacles. With a strong sense of self-esteem, we are more likely to step out of our comfort zone, seize opportunities and pursue personal growth.

Greater motivation

A healthy sense of pride is a powerful motivator. It propels us to set and achieve ambitious goals across various domains of our lives, be it our career, relationships or personal aspirations. Pride fuels our determination and our persistence in the face of difficulties.

Resilience

When setbacks and failures occur—as they inevitably do in each of our lives—pride serves as a protective shield for our emotional well-being. It provides the inner strength to bounce back from disappointments, learn from our mistakes and work hard towards our objectives. This resilience is also vital for maintaining a positive outlook, which helps us to bounce back from setbacks.

Improved relationships

And finally, a healthy sense of pride plays a pivotal role in improving our relationships with others. When we take pride in ourselves, we tend to radiate positivity, which, in turn, positively impacts our interactions with friends, family and colleagues. In relationships, this can lead to healthier and more fulfilling connections, as positivity fosters a sense of shared growth and celebration of each other's achievements.

How to cultivate healthy pride

Here are some strategies:

Acknowledge our strengths

First, we need to take purposeful moments to reflect on our unique qualities, talents and past achievements. Once we create a list of these attributes we revisit it regularly. This can even involve writing or updating our CV. Celebrating our strengths reinforces a positive self-image and helps us recognize the value we bring to various aspects of our lives. This self-affirmation can foster healthy pride.

Set achievable goals

We need to establish goals that challenge us but are realistically attainable. As we work towards these objectives, each milestone we reach becomes an opportunity for celebration. By acknowledging our progress and accomplishments, we can genuinely feel proud of our efforts and achievements without veering into arrogance.

Show ourselves compassion

Understand that making mistakes and experiencing setbacks are a part of life. Instead of indulging in harsh self-criticism, we should treat ourselves with kindness and empathy when facing challenges. Embracing self-compassion will let us maintain a healthy perspective, even during difficult times, and prevent pride from morphing into haughtiness.

Curate our social environment

We will always have two kinds of people in our life: those who see the good in us and appreciate us, and those who will criticise us for everything. We must surround ourselves with individuals who uplift us and seek out positive influences that encourage us to grow. At the same time, we must avoid those who constantly undermine our self-esteem or create negative feelings. A supportive social circle can help us maintain humility and nurture healthy pride.

Why humble leaders succeed?

"The greatest leader is not necessarily the one who does the greatest things. He is the one that gets the people to do the greatest things."—Ronald Reagan

Leadership has traditionally been associated with a strong and assertive personality. A leader is someone who commands respect and inspires awe in their subordinates. However, in recent years, respect for a new kind of leadership has emerged—humble leadership, which is now seen as an effective leadership style that can drive success in organizations. Humble leaders are not flashy or attention-seeking instead they lead by example and put the needs of their team ahead of their own. Such leaders inspire trust and foster a culture of innovation, creativity and continuous improvement. Let us explore why humble leaders succeed and the qualities that make them stand out.

Humble leaders are authentic

Humble leaders are honest about their strengths and weaknesses and are not afraid to admit when they do not have all the answers. This authenticity helps them build trust and credibility with their teams, which is essential for effective leadership.

Humble leaders empower their teams

Humble leaders understand that their success is tied to the success of their teams. They are not interested in micromanaging or controlling their team members instead they empower them to take ownership of their work and make decisions. Humble leaders understand that their role is to provide guidance, support and resources to their teams, rather than dictating what they should do.

Humble leaders prioritize learning and growth

Humble leaders understand that leadership is a journey and that there is always room for improvement. They seek out feedback from others, including their teams, peers and mentors, to identify areas for improvement, and are also open to new ideas and perspectives.

Humble leaders are great listeners

By actively listening to their team, humble leaders create an environment where everyone feels valued and heard, which in turn leads to a more engaged and motivated workforce.

Humble leaders take ownership of their actions

Humble leaders are not afraid to take responsibility for their actions, including their mistakes and failures, for they understand that their setbacks can be valuable learning experiences. By acknowledging their own weaknesses, they set an example for their team members to do the same, creating a culture of transparency and trust in the organization.

Humble leaders create a sense of purpose

Humble leaders understand that people are not just motivated by financial incentives, but also by a sense of belonging and a feeling that their work is making a positive impact on the world. By communicating a clear vision and values to their team, they create a shared sense of purpose that inspires everyone to work towards a common goal.

Humble leaders are great at building relationships

Humble leaders know that leadership is not just about giving orders, but also about developing meaningful connections with their team members. They take the time to get to know each person on an individual level, and they show genuine interest in their lives and their aspirations. This creates a sense of camaraderie and trust within the team, which in turn leads to higher levels of collaboration and productivity.

Hence, humble leaders prioritize leading by example, active listening, admitting mistakes, delegating, creating purpose and building strong relationships. They put their team's needs first, and while they may not be as charismatic as more conventional leaders, they are highly effective, well-liked and respected in their fraternity and world at large.

Conclusion

Hence, humility holds immense value in both personal and professional lives—which is why it is one of the 8-H principles. In personal interactions, it fosters empathy, openness to others' perspectives, and the ability to admit and learn from mistakes, strengthening relationships and promoting harmony. Professionally, humility enables leaders to inspire trust, collaboration and a sense of purpose among team members, leading to increased productivity and innovation. Embracing humility cultivates an environment of respect, understanding and genuine connections, enriching both personal well-being and professional achievements.

7 HUMANITY

"If we have no peace, it is because we have forgotten that we belong to each other." —Mother Teresa

On 11 March 2011, on an otherwise quiet late-winter afternoon, Japan was jolted by an earthquake measuring 9.1 on the Richter scale. Thousands perished as a result of this quake, one of the strongest ever recorded on earth, and a massive tsunami inundated the Fukushima Daiichi nuclear power plant, resulting in grid failure and complete damage to the plant's backup energy sources. Soon, radioactive material from the plant leaked into the surrounding environment, leading to a serious nuclear accident.

The crisis needed to be tackled so that it did not go out of control. A group of more than 200 elderly Japanese pensioners volunteered to tackle the nuclear crisis at the power station. The Skilled Veterans Corps, as they called themselves, was made up of retired engineers and other professionals, all over the age of sixty. They said they should be facing the dangers of radiation, not the young.

It was while watching the television news that this idea came to Yasuteru Yamada. A resolute decision stirred within him— to awaken his generation. No longer could he remain a passive observer in the struggle to stabilize the nuclear plant. At the age of seventy-two, this retired engineer resurfaced to answer the call of duty, assembling a team comprising fellow pensioners. Over weeks, Yamada reached out to old acquaintances through emails and even ventured into the realm of X, formerly called Twitter.

In Yamada's eyes, volunteering to replace younger workers at the power station was not an act of bravery, but rather a manifestation of sheer logic.

"At seventy-two, with an estimated 13 to 15 years left in my life," he said, "even if I were to be exposed to radiation, the onset of cancer could require twenty, thirty or perhaps even more years to manifest. Therefore, us older ones have less chance of getting cancer."

This is not just a story of bravery in the face of crisis or rising up to the occasion. This is a story of being humane. By being humane, we enrich lives, promote understanding, and contribute to a more compassionate and empathetic world.

What does it mean to be humane?

In a world where cut-throat competition seems to have permeated every aspect of our lives, it can be easy to forget the importance of being humane. But what does it mean to be humane? At its core, being humane is about treating others with compassion, kindness and respect. It is about recognizing the inherent value of every living being and striving to create a world where all individuals are able to live with dignity and security. When we treat others with kindness and respect, we feel better about ourselves. By becoming more connected to others, we experience a bigger sense of purpose. In this chapter, we will explore what it is like being humane and its significance in our personal and collective lives.

Being humane is a critical virtue because it promotes peace and harmony. When we treat others with kindness and respect, we create a positive and welcoming environment where people feel safe and supported. This, in turn, fosters a sense of belonging and encourages individuals to be their best selves. When people feel accepted and valued, they are more likely to work together and contribute positively to society.

Being humane also promotes social justice and equality. When we treat others with kindness and respect, we are more likely to recognize and address social injustices and inequalities. We become more aware of the struggles that others face and are more likely to take action to address them. By being humane, we promote fairness and equality for all, regardless of their background or circumstances.

Being humane is critical also because it promotes a healthier and more sustainable world. When we treat animals and the environment with kindness and respect, we become more aware of the impact that our actions have on the world around us. We are more likely to adopt sustainable and ethical practices that promote the well-being of the planet and its inhabitants. By being humane, we promote a more sustainable and liveable world for ourselves and the future generations.

Different people and cultures may have varying definitions and interpretations of the concept of being humane. For example, in Western cultures, being humane is closely linked with the idea of human rights and the treatment of individuals with dignity and respect. In contrast, some Eastern cultures place more emphasis on the idea of harmony and balance between all living beings, and being humane involves showing respect and compassion towards animals and the environment.

Religious and philosophical traditions can also shape ideas about what it means to be humane. For example, the concept of "ahimsa" or non-violence is an important principle in Jainism and Hinduism and involves avoiding harm to all living beings. In Buddhism, the idea of *metta* or loving-kindness is central and involves developing compassion towards all sentient beings.

Habits to cultivate for being humane

By practising some of the following habits regularly, we can become more compassionate, caring and understanding:

Empathy

The ability to understand and share the feelings of others is the foundation of being humane. We can improve our empathy by practising active listening, that is, paying attention to the person speaking and trying to understand their perspective. It also involves asking questions and clarifying any misunderstanding. When we practise empathy, we develop a deeper connection with others and improve our ability to be humane.

Compassion

Compassion is a deep concern for the welfare of others, including their physical, emotional and mental well-being.

Kindness

Even the smallest acts of kindness—such as holding the door open for someone, smiling or offering a compliment—can make a big difference in someone's day. This extends to avoiding causing harm to animals and providing them with appropriate care, including adequate food, water and shelter.

Forgiveness

Holding grudges and being unforgiving can make one bitter and resentful. We must learn to let go of grudges and forgive others, even when it is difficult.

Respect and tolerance

Humane behaviour involves accepting and appreciating differences in race, religion, culture, gender, sexual orientation and more. This is one of the foundational principles of a peaceful and equitable society.

Gratitude

Being thankful for what we have is a powerful way to cultivate positivity. When we practise gratitude, we focus on the good things in our lives, and this can help us be more compassionate towards others.

Self-awareness

The ability to recognize our own emotions, thoughts and biases is a crucial step towards being more humane. When we are self-aware, we can recognize when we are being unkind or judgemental towards others. We can also identify our triggers and work on managing our emotions in a more positive way.

Responsibility

Taking responsibility for our actions and the consequences that come with them is also an essential part of being humane.

Growth mindset

A growth mindset is a belief that we can improve ourselves through effort and learning. When we have such a mindset, we are more open to feedback and criticism and we see challenges as opportunities to learn and grow. This way we can be more compassionate towards others because we recognize that everyone has the potential to improve themselves.

The environment

Humane behaviour also involves taking steps to protect the environment, such as reducing waste, recycling, conserving resources and using eco-friendly products.

Speaking up

An important aspect of being humane involves speaking up against wrongdoing. It also includes advocating for the rights of those who are mistreated or marginalized, whether that be animals or humans.

Essential characteristics of being humane

Empathy, kindness and tolerance are three of the most critical traits that define humanity. These virtues allow us to connect with others on a deeper level, understand their perspectives and build strong, meaningful relationships. In today's fast-paced world, where individualism and self-interest often take centre stage, it is easy to lose sight of the importance of these values. However, they remain essential in creating a better world for ourselves and future generations. Here we will explore each of these characteristics in more detail, examining why they are essential for a humane society and how we can cultivate them in ourselves and others. We will also explore the challenges and obstacles that can prevent us from embodying these qualities, and how we can overcome them to become better individuals.

Empathy

Empathy is an essential trait for building strong relationships, resolving conflicts and fostering a sense of community. It allows us to connect with others on a personal level, recognize their needs, and respond with kindness and understanding.

In 1938, Nicholas Winton was a young British stockbroker who was planning to go on a skiing vacation in Switzerland. However, a friend asked him to cancel his plans and come to Prague to help with the refugee crisis there. Winton agreed to go and was horrified by what he saw. Thousands of Jews were fleeing Nazi Germany and Austria, and many of them were stuck in refugee camps in Czechoslovakia (now the Czech Republic and Slovakia). Winton decided to take action and began organizing trains to take Jewish children to safety in England.

Over the course of several months, Winton organized eight trains and rescued 669 children, many of whose parents perished in Nazi concentration camps. He found British families to take them in, arranged for their travel documents and even went door to door to raise funds for the rescue mission.

Nicholas Winton's story is a beautiful example of how one person's empathy and action can make a huge difference in the lives of others. It is a reminder that even in the darkest of times, hope and kindness can always prevail. One of the most beautiful aspects of Winton's story is his humility. He almost never spoke of his heroic actions, and it was not until half a century later that his wife discovered a scrapbook in their attic with all of the details of the rescue mission. She brought it to the attention of the media, and Nicholas Winton was finally recognized for his tremendous acts of empathy and bravery.

Kindness

Kindness is an essential characteristic of a humane person. Being kind means acting in a way that uplifts others, spreads positivity and makes the world a better place. Kindness can take many forms, from a simple smile or a compliment to a grand gesture of generosity. It is also an essential trait for building trust, fostering friendships and creating a sense of belonging.

Kindness extends beyond fellow-feeling for humans. One prominent example can be found in the story of Henry Bergh, an American diplomat and failed-playwright-turned-philanthropist, who is widely recognized as the founder of the American Society for the Prevention of Cruelty to Animals (ASPCA) in 1866. The late nineteenth century marked a pivotal shift in the relationship between humans and animals in the United States. Bergh, eccentric and wealthy, played a central role in this transformation, passionately declaring that ending cruelty to animals was not only possible but also necessary. Bergh's actions ignited a reform movement that addressed moral questions about our treatment of animals.

Despite starting this mission late in life, at age fifty-three, Bergh dedicated himself to battling thoughtless cruelty. Always impeccably dressed, often adorned with a top hat and a silver-headed cane, he fearlessly ventured into grim corners of New York that few of his social status had ever dared to explore. His missions led him to raid saloons to quell dogfights and rat-baiting contests. He apprehended turtle dealers who subjected these creatures to painfully inhumane treatment, even presenting some unfortunate turtles as evidence in court. He did not discriminate based on wealth or status, chastising the elite for their fox hunts and pigeon shooting tournaments and disrupting the daily routines of New Yorkers when he discovered trolley horses being overworked.

Bergh's efforts garnered both admiration and ridicule. Some saw him as overly obsessed with the welfare of animals, while others resented his interference with what they considered their personal property. Nevertheless, he became a famous and notorious figure, known as "the man who is kind to animals".

Bergh was not alone in his quest. Across the United States, countless individuals joined forces, forming local societies for the Prevention of Cruelty to Animals and other organizations to protect animals from abuse. They established the first shelters, advocated for laws to reduce animal suffering during transportation and slaughter, and initiated the battle against animal experimentation. Together, they worked tirelessly to make kindness to animals an integral part of education and society. Bergh's causes reverberate in today's questions about human ethics and the role of kindness in our daily lives.

Tolerance

Tolerance is an essential characteristic of a humane individual. It means accepting and respecting the beliefs, values and opinions of others, which may be different from our own. Tolerance requires an open mind and a willingness to listen to different perspectives without judgement or prejudice. It is essential for creating a diverse and inclusive society where everyone feels valued and respected, and is a fundamental aspect of humanism, which emphasizes the worth and dignity of all human beings.

Looking at the history of the Western world, one notable example of tolerance is the "Edict of Milan". Issued in the year 313 AD by the Roman emperors Constantine the Great and Licinius, this edict can be seen as a significant milestone in the history of religious tolerance. During that time, the Roman Empire was characterized by great religious diversity, the Romans being primarily a polytheistic civilization, which meant that people recognized and worshipped multiple gods and goddesses. But Christianity was emerging as a prominent faith and Christians faced periods of persecution under various Roman emperors. However, Constantine and Licinius, in an effort to stabilize the empire and end religious conflict, issued the Edict of Milan.

The edict proclaimed religious tolerance throughout the Roman Empire, granting Christians and all other religious groups the right to freely practise their faith without fear of oppression or discrimination. Constantine's decision to promote religious tolerance was influenced by his own conversion to Christianity and his desire to unify the empire under a policy of religious coexistence. This historical example of tolerance demonstrates the potential for leaders to promote harmony and coexistence among diverse religious groups, fostering an environment where people can live peacefully and prosper. The Edict of Milan played a pivotal role in the evolution of religious freedom and tolerance in the Western world, leaving a lasting legacy that continues to influence discussions on religious liberty today.

Closer home, a powerful example of tolerance from Indian history is the reign of Mughal Emperor Akbar during the sixteenth century. During his rule, Akbar not only practised his own religion, Islam, but also actively sought to understand and respect the beliefs of people from various faiths, including Hinduism, Christianity, Jainism, Sikhism and Buddhism, among others. His progressive policies promoted religious tolerance in a diverse and culturally rich empire.

One of his most significant acts of religious tolerance was the issuance of the "Ibadat Khana" (House of Worship) decree in 1575. This edict encouraged open discussions on religious matters and welcomed scholars from different faiths to participate. Akbar believed that through dialogue and understanding, people of diverse religious backgrounds could coexist peacefully. Furthermore, Akbar implemented policies that ensured the protection and fair treatment of religious minorities in his empire. He abolished the jizya tax imposed on non-Muslims, allowed people to practise their faith without fear of persecution, married women of different faiths who could continue worshipping their own gods and even appointed individuals from different religious backgrounds to high-ranking positions in his government.

Akbar's commitment to religious tolerance fostered a sense of unity and harmony among his subjects, creating an era of peace and prosperity in the Mughal Empire. His legacy as a tolerant ruler is remembered as a shining example of how embracing diversity and respecting different beliefs can lead to social unity and progress.

All these virtues share related traits. Let us break down the characteristics that are common to empathy, kindness and tolerance.

Having an understanding nature

We must put ourselves in someone else's shoes and understand their point of view, even if it differs from ours. This requires an open mind to truly comprehend what someone else is feeling.

Sharing feelings

It goes beyond just understanding another person's feelings. It also involves being able to share those emotions and respond appropriately, such as providing support, comfort or simply acknowledging the other person's feelings.

Being non-judgemental

Being non-judgemental means not making assumptions or jumping to conclusions about someone's emotions or behaviours. Instead, it involves being open to hearing their story and understanding their experiences.

Being caring

Caring about another person's well-being and wanting to alleviate their suffering is central to all these qualities.

Being generous

Giving time, resources or emotional support is also central. A kind and compassionate person is willing to share what they have and help others in need.

Being humble

We must act out of a genuine desire to help others and make the world a better place. The motivation must not be a want for recognition or praise for our kind actions.

Being patient

Tolerant individuals are patient and understanding, recognizing that change takes time and effort.

Being present

Finally, all these qualities demand putting aside distractions and being fully present in the moment and giving our full attention to the other person.

A few important cases of intolerance

Tolerance can refer to different things in different contexts. Social tolerance involves the acceptance of diverse social groups along with their beliefs, practices and ways of life, irrespective of characteristics such as race, religion, gender identity, sexual orientation or political affiliation.

Political tolerance means a willingness to permit individuals with differing political perspectives to voice their opinions and engage in the political sphere, demonstrating respect for their right to hold contrasting viewpoints.

Similarly, religious tolerance entails embracing a variety of faiths, beliefs and practices, showing respect for individuals' freedom to adhere to their chosen religion or belief system without the threat of persecution or bias.

Intolerance is the opposite of tolerance, where someone displays a lack of respect or acceptance towards a person or group who is different from them in some way. It manifests in many forms, including discrimination, prejudice, bigotry and hatred. Human intolerance has been a pervasive issue throughout our history, leading to countless instances of discrimination, oppression and violence. A few gruesome instances:

The transatlantic slave trade

One of the most far-reaching instances of historical intolerance might be the transatlantic slave trade, also called the triangular trade, which operated from the fifteenth to the mid-nineteenth century. Enslaved Africans were transported across the Atlantic Ocean to the Americas in brutal conditions, with the same ships carrying back goods from Europe to Africa for trade. Africans suffered inhumane treatment during the journey, and once in the Americas, they endured harsh labour and punishment. This trade fuelled cash-crop economies in the Americas and Europe, aiding the Industrial Revolution. The lasting consequences of this brutal practice include profound impacts on African societies and cultures, and the persistence of slavery's legacy shaping social and political dynamics in the Americas.

The Rwandan genocide

More recent examples of intolerance include the 1994 Rwandan genocide. It was a brutal massacre of Tutsi and moderate Hutu people that resulted from longstanding ethnic tensions, political strife and economic issues. Before the violence, the Tutsi community were marginalized under a Hutu-dominated government. A civil war erupted in 1990 with the armed insurrection by the Tutsi-led Rwandan Patriotic Front (RPF). Despite a peace accord, extremist Hutus orchestrated the genocide after the assassination of the country's president. In just 100 days, up to one million Tutsis and moderate Hutus were killed by militias and civilians. The international response was slow, and it was not until the RPF's victory in July 1994 that the violence ended. The aftermath underscored the importance of reconciliation, ethnic unity and international intervention in preventing genocide.

The Great Bengal Famine

Closer home, we must not forget the Great Famine of Bengal, which remains a harrowing emblem of British imperial cruelty. The 1943 Bengal Famine, intensified by World War II, saw the once-fertile Bengal transform into a wasteland of death. Millions suffered from starvation and disease due to food shortages, worsened by the Japanese occupation of Burma and a criminally negligent colonial government. The British Empire exacerbated the tragedy by exporting Indian food for its own war needs. Despite the desperate cries of the afflicted, relief efforts were meagre, with bureaucratic hurdles and obstruction abounding. This heartless colonial exploitation caused an estimated 2 to 3 million deaths. The famine's impact reverberated throughout Bengal, decimating villages and pushing city dwellers to scavenge for sustenance. The catastrophe is a poignant testament to the perils of inhumane colonialism, as well as the resilience of survivors, and a call to remember the consequences of apathy and greed in the face of human suffering.

India's intolerance: a blemish on its pluralistic tapestry

India, a land of diverse cultures, languages and traditions, has been marred by incidents of intolerance and bigotry over the years. Despite the country's rich history of inclusivity and pluralism, there have been many instances of communal violence, hate speech and discrimination against certain groups based on their religion, caste, gender or sexual orientation. Amid the bustling crowds of our vibrant cities, town and villages, an insidious undercurrent of intolerance is often felt, seeping through the cracks of the nation's complex social fabric.

Historically, Indian women have endured discrimination, violence and practices such as sati, dowry and female infanticide. Despite recent progress, challenges persist in areas of women's mobility, education and employment, let alone the scourge of rape and sexual exploitation. The rigid caste system perpetuates inequalities and injustices with discrimination, violence and exploitation against underprivileged castes. Religious divisions also fuel intolerance with Hindus, Muslims, Sikhs and Christians often clashing with one another, sometimes abetted by politics of division. The LGBTQ+ community also faced discrimination and criminalization until 2018, when the colonial-era Section 377 was repealed, yet prejudice lingers. These issues underscore the ongoing struggle against deep-rooted prejudices and inequalities in India.

Why is there so much intolerance?

The above few stories of historic intolerance serve as reminders of the grave consequences of hatred and discrimination. They highlight the need to foster tolerance, understanding and respect for human dignity so that we can become a more humane society. But what are the roots of intolerance to begin with? Unless we understand them, there can be no moving forward.

We can break down some of the reasons for intolerance as follows:

Lack of education

Proper, holistic education plays a significant role in shaping an individual's mindset. If the education system does not promote a tolerant attitude towards people of different cultures, races, or religions, it will create intolerant minds.

Fear and insecurity

When people feel threatened by someone who is different from them, they develop prejudice and intolerance towards that person—and by extension, an entire group of people.

Historical factors

History also counts. If a country, for instance, has a history of colonization or imperialism, it can lead to resentment towards the people of the colonizing country. Similarly, histories of invasion and past persecution of certain communities also lead to distaste and resentment among people in the present.

Political factors

Propaganda, nationalism and populism can also contribute to intolerance. It is possible for political leaders to use these tactics to create a sense of unity among people, but it can also lead to an "us vs them" mentality that fosters intolerance.

Religious and cultural differences

When people believe that their religious and cultural way of life is superior to others, such beliefs become a recipe for intolerance towards those who are from different religious communities or those whose actions are not approved by certain religions.

Economic factors

Economic inequality and competition for resources can also contribute to intolerance, as people may view those who are different as a threat to their own economic well-being.

Barriers to being humane

As social beings, we are inherently wired to care for others, to empathize and to be kind. However, there are times when we fail to live up to these ideals. It helps to explore some of the barriers to being humane and suggest ways in which we can overcome them.

Biases

Biases are preconceived notions or attitudes towards certain groups of people. These biases can be conscious or unconscious and can be based on factors such as race, gender, sexual orientation, religion or socioeconomic status. Biases can prevent us from seeing people as individuals and treating them with the respect they deserve. For example, a doctor may not give the same level of care to a patient whom they perceive to be of a lower socioeconomic status than a patient whom they perceive to be wealthier.

Prejudices

Prejudices are negative attitudes or beliefs about certain groups of people. These can easily lead to discrimination and can prevent us from treating people with kindness and compassion. For example, someone who holds prejudices against immigrants is less likely to offer help to a person who is struggling due to their immigration status.

Self-interest

Self-interest is the focus on our own needs or desires rather than the needs of others, preventing us from being empathetic and compassionate towards others. For example, a business owner may prioritize profits over the well-being of their employees, thereby creating dissatisfaction among the staff.

Strategies for overcoming barriers to being humane

Educate ourselves

To overcome biases and prejudices, it is important to educate ourselves about different cultures, beliefs and perspectives. This requires a willingness to confront our own biases and prejudices, challenge them and actively seek out diverse experiences. We can do this by engaging in conversations with people from different backgrounds, reading books and articles written by diverse authors, and attending events and workshops that promote diversity and inclusion.

Engage in self-reflection

Self-reflection helps us recognize our biases, prejudices and levels of self-interest, and work towards overcoming them. This can be done through journaling, meditation or seeking feedback from others.

Take action

Overcoming barriers to being humane requires action. This includes volunteering, donating to charitable causes or advocating for social justice. It is important to take action that aligns with our values and beliefs and to be persistent in the face of challenges or setbacks.

Practise empathy

This can help us overcome self-interest and better understand the needs of others. We can practise empathy by actively listening to others and trying to see things from their perspective.

Being humane requires a conscious effort to recognize these barriers and to work towards overcoming them. As Mahatma Gandhi once said, "The true measure of any society can be found in how it treats its most vulnerable members." It is our duty to create a society that is truly humane, kind and compassionate towards all.

How to be humane in the different spheres of our lives

In this book, I have focused on the practical aspects of the 8-H principles. Just like the other qualities discussed in this book, being humane has a significant impact on the quality of our lives, be it in the workplace, in personal relationships or in society in general. Let us dwell on how humaneness can be practised in these aspects of our lives.

In the workplace

Fostering a culture of respect and kindness is essential for a harmonious environment in the workplace. Treating colleagues with genuine consideration creates a sense of belonging, boosts morale and promotes collaborative teamwork, ultimately leading to increased productivity and job satisfaction.

Recognizing and valuing diversity and inclusion not only enriches the work atmosphere, but also enhances creativity and innovation. Employing people from a variety of backgrounds generates fresh ideas, encourages critical thinking and propels the organization forward in an evolving global landscape.

Providing support and resources for employees to maintain work-life balance is crucial. This involves allowing flexible schedules, offering wellness programmes and encouraging time

Expressing appreciation and gratitude for each other's contributions fuels positivity and affirmation, creating a sense of validation and acknowledgement that enhances harmony in a relationship.

In society as a whole

Practising empathy and understanding bridges divides, fostering unity among diverse backgrounds and promoting a sense of shared humanity that transcends cultural differences.

Advocating for social justice and equality is important to combat systemic injustices, ensuring that every individual has a fair and equal opportunity to thrive, and contribute to a more just and inclusive society.

Valuing and respecting the rights of all individuals, regardless of race, gender, sexuality, religion or ability, upholds the principles of human dignity and promotes harmonious coexistence.

Showing kindness and generosity to those in need reflects the essence of a compassionate society, extending a helping hand to vulnerable individuals, and fostering a culture of mutual support and care that strengthens the social fabric.

Promoting sustainability and environmental responsibility safeguards our planet's future, acknowledging our collective responsibility to preserve natural resources and minimize ecological harm for the well-being of the present and future generations.

Steps towards a sustainable future

Amidst the cacophony of daily life, there is a rising chorus that cannot be ignored—the wail of a planet in peril. As carbon emissions reach record highs, temperatures soar, ice melts and sea levels rise, the earth's ecosystems are buckling under the strain. The urgency of the situation cannot be overstated—the very future of life as we know it hangs in the balance.

But as we grapple with the enormity of this challenge, we must remember that this is not just an ecological crisis, but a humanitarian one. Climate change does not discriminate—it affects rich and poor, young and old, human and animal alike. It exacerbates poverty, hunger and displacement, and threatens the fundamental human rights of millions around the world.

A humane approach to climate change means acknowledging the interconnectedness of all life on this planet. It means recognizing that the fate of the natural world and the fate of humanity are inextricably linked. It means understanding that our actions have consequences, and that we have a responsibility to each other and the future generations to act with compassion and foresight.

This compassionate response begins with acknowledging the disproportionate impact of climate change on vulnerable populations, such as indigenous peoples, women and children. It means including their voices and experiences in our discussions and decisions, and recognizing their right to a safe and sustainable future.

It also means recognizing the immense power we have as individuals and communities to effect change. We can choose to consume responsibly, reduce our carbon footprint, and advocate for policies that prioritize the health of the planet and its inhabitants. We can support sustainable agriculture, renewable energy, and conservation efforts that protect and restore the natural world.

Reducing our carbon footprint and contributing towards a greener planet is not only a responsibility, but also an opportunity to make a positive impact on the world. Even small steps taken in this direction can go a long way in mitigating the effects of global warming and reducing carbon emissions. Here are some small yet impactful steps that we can take to go green and contribute towards a sustainable future:

Use public transport

Using public transport instead of private vehicles reduces the number of cars on the road, leading to fewer emissions and less air pollution. For short distances, walking or biking can be a great way to not only reduce carbon emissions but also improve our health and well-being. Alternatively, taking public transportation or carpooling with colleagues or friends can help reduce the number of cars on the road, which can have a significant impact on carbon emissions.

Save water

Conserving water is a crucial aspect of going green. Simple steps like turning off the tap while brushing teeth, fixing leaks, using low-flow showerheads and reusing water can significantly reduce water consumption and save a very precious and fast-depleting resource.

Eat local and sustainable

Our food choices also have a significant impact on the environment. Eating locally sourced and sustainable food reduces the carbon footprint of the food we consume. Especially in Western countries, plant-based diets also reduce the greenhouse gas emissions associated with meat production.

Reduce plastic use

Plastic pollution is a major environmental concern and reducing our plastic usage can make a significant difference. Adopting reusable bags, water bottles and containers, avoiding single-use plastic products and properly disposing of plastic waste are some small steps towards reducing plastic usage.

Use electronic means

We can reduce our paper usage by switching to e-cards and digital communication instead of printed materials. This way we can reduce our carbon footprint and help protect the world's forests, which are vital for regulating the earth's climate.

Use energy-efficient light bulbs

One of the easiest and most effective steps towards going green is to switch to energy-efficient light bulbs such as LED lights. These bulbs not only consume less energy but also have a longer lifespan, making them a cost-effective option in the long run.

Use renewable energy

Investing in renewable energy sources like solar panels, wind turbines or hydroelectric power can significantly reduce our reliance on fossil fuels and contribute to a cleaner environment. While not possible for everyone, it is good to support local or national renewable energy initiatives and switch to green energy suppliers.

Plant local trees

Planting trees is one of the most effective ways to reduce carbon emissions and combat climate change. Trees absorb carbon dioxide and other pollutants, release oxygen and help in reducing air pollution. Planting trees in your backyard, supporting local tree-planting initiatives or even sponsoring tree-planting campaigns can make a positive impact. Make sure that you plant and support planting of trees that are indigenous to the local environment, so that they can sustain the necessary ecosystem.

Gift green

Gifting plants has become a popular trend due to their visual appeal and numerous health benefits. This practice, now common on occasions like birthdays and work anniversaries, symbolizes appreciation and care. Amidst a tech-driven world, tending to plants offers a respite, enhancing air quality, reducing stress and boosting productivity. Plants in workplaces elevate job satisfaction and well-being, making them more than just decorative elements.

But ultimately, a humane approach to climate change requires a fundamental shift in our worldview. We must move beyond the narrow confines of individualism and consumerism and embrace a vision of interconnectedness and collective responsibility. We must recognize that our well-being is intimately tied to the well-being of the planet and all its inhabitants, and that true prosperity cannot be achieved at the expense of the natural world.

The urgency of the climate crisis demands nothing less than a radical reimagining of our relationship with the earth and with each other. It calls for a new paradigm of empathy, compassion and shared responsibility. Let us heed the cry of the planet and respond with the fullness of our humanity.

Conclusion

There is no quality more central to our existence than being human. This is why we have explored the virtue of humanity towards the end of our survey of the 8-H Principle. When we are kind, we create inclusive, secure environments, nurturing a sense of belonging that motivates individuals to achieve their potential and contribute positively to society. When we are compassionate and treat others with benevolence, we spread awareness of social injustices and inspire action to right social wrongs.

What is more, our humaneness is pivotal for a healthier, more sustainable world. Conscientious treatment of animals and the environment and awareness of our actions' global impact lead to sustainable, ethical practices that prioritize the well-being of our planet, which we all call home. By embracing our own humanity, our core values, we advocate for a more habitable world for present and future generations.

8 HOPE

> "Hope is the only bee that makes honey without flowers."
> —Robert Green Ingersoll

Nick Vujicic was born on 4 December 1982 in Melbourne, Australia, with tetra-amelia syndrome (TETAMS), a rare disorder characterized by the absence of arms and legs.

Nick's parents were both immigrants from Serbia, and they were devastated by their son's condition. However, they decided to raise Nick like any other child and encouraged him to live a normal life. Nick faced many challenges growing up, but he was determined to overcome them.

As a child, Nick struggled to cope with his physical limitations. He was bullied and teased by other children at school. Feeling isolated and alone, he struggled with depression and even tried to attempt suicide at the age of ten. However, he eventually found hope and purpose through his Christian faith. He learned to do everyday tasks using his mouth and toes, and went on to earn a bachelor's degree in commerce from Griffith University.

Nick discovered his passion for public speaking when he was a teenager and began sharing his story with others. As he grew older, he became determined to inspire and motivate others who were facing similar challenges. He started speaking to small groups of people about his experiences and how he had overcome his limitations. In 2005, he founded his own evangelical organization, Life Without Limbs, with the aim to provide support and encouragement to people with disabilities.

Nick's message of hope and resilience has touched the lives of millions. He has travelled to seventy-eight countries, sharing his story and inspiring others to overcome their own challenges. He has also written several books, including his memoir *Life Without Limits: Inspiration for a Ridiculously Good Life*. Nick is married to Kanae Miyahara, and they have four children. He believes that everyone has something to offer the world, regardless of their physical or emotional challenges. He continues to inspire people around the world with his message of hope and perseverance.

The power of hope

Hope is one of the most powerful emotions in our lives, which is precisely why I have included this as one of the 8-H principles. The potent force of hope is evident in those who triumph over immense challenges to achieve their goals. Hope drives scientists, inventors, athletes and entrepreneurs to success, providing motivation to struggle through setbacks and maintain a positive attitude. It is an enigmatic force, a beacon of light that illuminates the dark and uncertain moments in our lives, infusing our spirit with the belief that the future holds a promise of better things to come.

Hope provides us with a sense of purpose, a reason to believe that we can overcome the obstacles that lie in our path. When we have hope, we have something to strive for, a reason to keep moving forward even when the road ahead seems uncertain. It gives us the strength to carry on, to face our challenges head-on and to push through difficult times.

Research links hope to improved mental health, fostering resilience, optimism and life satisfaction, and even helping in the management of stress and anxiety. What is more, hope strengthens relationships, builds trust, connection and forgiveness. On a societal level, too, hope inspires change by sparking revolutions, promoting social justice and uniting people to achieve remarkable feats, such as building fair and equal societies.

Hope is a lifeline in a time of crisis. Amid the Covid-19 pandemic, for example, hope united people, providing strength to face challenges together. It fuelled efforts for vaccine development, inspiring global collaboration among scientists. Hope emerged as a force that brought common people and governments together and helped us support one another during those immensely troubling times.

However, hope is not a magic cure-all; it cannot solve all our problems or make all our dreams come true. It is neither a guarantee of success, nor is it a shield against failure. Hope can be fragile, it can be shattered by setbacks and disappointments, and it can be lost altogether if we do not nurture it. We need to learn to balance hope with realism, to temper our expectations with an understanding of the challenges that lie ahead.

The art of nurturing a culture of positivity

Hope is not a passive emotion—it requires action, effort and a willingness to take risks. Hope without action is merely wishful thinking, but hope combined with action can lead to powerful outcomes. Can we learn to cultivate hope and create a positive environment that nurtures it?

The answer is yes. Even though hope can be passive, it is not a static emotion. It is a dynamic state of mind that can be cultivated and nurtured through intentional practice. Like a seed that needs fertile soil, sunlight and water to grow into a beautiful plant, hope needs the right environment to flourish. The art of cultivating hope is a practise of the soul that requires patience, persistence and faith. It is a journey that can inspire us to become the best version of ourselves and contribute to the well-being of the world.

But how to cultivate hope?

Acknowledge our fears, doubts and worries

Confront the shadows that haunt our minds and hearts and embrace them with compassion and courage. Face our vulnerabilities and weaknesses with honesty and transform them into sources of strength and resilience.

Focus on the positive aspects of life

We should try not to dwell on the negatives in our lives and the world around us. This does not mean that we ignore the challenges we face or deny the realities of our circumstances instead, it implies that we actively seek out the good and the possibilities that exist within them.

Practise gratitude

When we focus on what we have, rather than what we lack, we shift our perspective and begin to see the world through a different lens. So, be thankful for the blessings in your life.

Practise forgiveness

We can arrive at hope by letting go of resentments and grievances, and opening our heart to healing and reconciliation. We become more open to possibilities and are better able to bounce back from setbacks and challenges.

Put in collective effort

Creating a culture of hope requires us to support and encourage one another, lift each other up when we fall and celebrate each other's successes. Try and create a safe and inclusive environment where everyone feels valued and heard. When we share our hopes and dreams with others and listen to them in turn, we create a sense of community and belonging that is essential for nurturing hope.

Set realistic goals

If we set goals that are too ambitious or unrealistic, we can easily become discouraged when we fail to achieve them. This leads to a sense of hopelessness and a lack of motivation to continue striving for success. Celebrating small wins and acknowledging progress towards larger goals is another important aspect of developing a culture of hope.

Hope as therapy

> "We must accept finite disappointment, but never lose infinite hope."—Martin Luther King Jr.

The impact of hope and optimism on both physical and mental health has been a topic of discussion among scholars in recent years. Empirical evidence suggests that these attitudes contribute to positive outcomes. Optimism leads to reduced distress and richer daily life experiences, even in challenging situations. Optimists focus on general expectations rather than specific methods of goal achievement—and this has been associated with fewer symptoms of depression, greater well-being and stronger social support. Research shows that in the professional world, optimism leads to lower attrition rates, that is, people stay with their companies for a longer period of time.

Pessimists, on the other hand, end up engaging in riskier behaviours. C. R. Snyder, a renowned expert in positive psychology, said hope involves setting goals, planning pathways to achieve them, and possessing the motivation and confidence to follow through. It emphasizes personal agency and strategies for goal attainment. Research shows that hope is influenced by personality traits, psychosocial conditions and physiological as well as environmental factors.

Positive expectations for the future can act as potential mechanisms for achieving positive mental health. Multiple research papers by psychologists Matthew W. Gallagher and Shane J. Lopez have shown that hope can alleviate conditions such as depression, anxiety and trauma-related disorders. It has strong associations with positive affect, emotional adjustment and life satisfaction.

Studies among older people have shown that greater hope is linked to better physical health, reduced psychological distress and psychosocial well-being. A 2022 study by psychologists Carlos Laranjeira and Ana Querido suggests that hope-based interventions are crucial for mental health particularly in vulnerable populations. In a time when mental health challenges are prominent, evidence-based approaches that incorporate hope are essential for intervention and well-being.

Hope in the treatment of addictions

"The good physician treats the disease; the great physician treats the patient who has the disease."—William Osler

There is little doubt that substance abuse or drug addiction is a perilous path to follow. The relentless pursuit of drugs can consume one's life, causing a downward spiral that is very difficult to break free from. The dangers of drug addiction are not limited to the individual; they ripple through families and communities, exacting a heavy toll on society as a whole. Thankfully, substance abuse treatments exist and more and more people are able to access them.

In the past, when checking if substance abuse treatment worked, people mainly looked at how often and how much drugs a person used, and if they stopped using drugs. But nowadays, there has been a major change in how we think about addiction and recovery. Instead of just focusing on the problems caused by addiction, experts now consider a wider range of factors, like how well a person is doing in their life overall and how they feel about it. This shift means that we look at addiction and recovery more like aspects of a person's general health and happiness, rather than just as a problem to fix.

Hope has emerged as a significant psychological factor in addiction recovery, echoing the acknowledgement of hope as a catalyst for recovery by the Substance Abuse and Mental Health Services Administration (SAMHSA), the United States government body tasked with dealing with this issue.

There are three important aspects of being hopeful:
- believing we can do things,
- knowing how to do them and
- considering the situation around us.

When people have hope, it helps them stay motivated and figure out solutions to problems, especially when they are trying to recover from something like drug addiction. Research has shown that optimistic people can stay away from harmful habits for longer and generally have a better quality of life.

Having helpful and friendly surroundings is really important when someone is trying to overcome addiction. It is like being part of a group where everyone has a role to play. This group feeling has three aspects: what the group stands for, who is in the group and how much we personally care about the group. How we see the environment around us can make a big difference in how hopeful we feel. Empirical studies have shown that the environment accounts for approximately 50 per cent of an individual's hope levels in recovery homes.

Being part of a supportive group and having good relationships with others can help a person believe in themselves and their ability to stay away from harmful substances. It is really important to understand and work on these feelings of wellness, hope and being part of a group when trying to overcome addiction. By doing this, we can make sure that people have a greater chance of getting better and staying out of harm's way. In a 2018 study titled "Relationship of Hope, Sense of Community, and Quality of Life" published in the *Journal of Community Psychology*, a group of psychologists suggested that recognizing how hope affects a person and including it in treatment and support programmes can make the recovery process better and help people feel happier and healthier along the way.

Hope for better health for cancer patients

We are unfortunately familiar with the fact that cancer is one of the world's largest health problems. The *Global Burden of Disease* estimates that today up to ten million people die prematurely as a result of cancer every year. Some statistics even suggest that every sixth death in the world is due to cancer. While there have been significant advancements in cancer treatments, leading to a nominal reduction in cancer mortality, it is only to be expected that cancer patients often experience feelings of hopelessness, making them vulnerable to depression. Recognizing the need to address the positive aspects of care, the concept of hope has gained prominence in the treatment of cancer in recent years.

Hope in the context of cancer can be understood as a state of mind that involves a positive outlook on achieving tangible outcomes while maintaining a realistic understanding of potential negative outcomes. The concept of rehabilitating cancer patients acknowledges the complexity of the situation faced by cancer survivors, some of whom may have completed treatment while others continue to manage residual morbidity and fear of recurrence. Cancer rehabilitation aims to restore patients' physical and mental abilities.

Multiple studies have shown that hope can lead to positive changes in cancer patients, including improved quality of life and reduced symptoms such as depression, pain, fatigue and cough. The relevance of hope to cancer rehabilitation programmes is underscored by the prevalence of depression among cancer patients. Depression is often linked to hopelessness, and hope is seen as a protective factor against depression. Enhancing hope helps buffer against depressive symptoms and improve psychological well-being.

Hope in coping with traumatic events

Gunung Merapi or "Fire Mountain", located near the border of Central Java and the Special Region of Yogyakarta in Indonesia, is one of the most active volcanoes in the world. In late October 2010, it started erupting violently—and continued to erupt many times over the following five weeks, spewing out lava and volcanic ash. Huge columns of ash and smoke formed, and numerous pyroclastic flows descended down the volcano's slopes.

To keep people safe, more than 3,50,000 were moved away from the area that could be affected by the eruption. Some people, though, stayed in their homes or even returned while the volcano was still erupting. Sadly, 353 people lost their lives during these eruptions, mainly because of the dangerous lava flows. Additionally, the ash clouds from the volcano caused significant problems for planes flying over Java, leading to travel disruptions. This disaster had extensive environmental and societal impacts, including damage to settlements, public infrastructure and the economy. It also pushed more people into poverty, leading to shifts in social strata.

For instance, the residents of Sirahan Village, primarily farmers, lost their main source of livelihood as their lands were covered by volcanic materials. Additionally, they struggled to secure funds for starting new businesses and rebuilding their economic life. The impacts of the disaster extended beyond the physical realm and included psychological repercussions. Survivors experienced ongoing trauma, exacerbated by their prolonged stay in refugee camps and temporary shelters. Even those who returned home remained haunted by anxiety, especially at times when the sky appeared cloudy. Psychological symptoms such as decreased consciousness, amnesia, sadness, distress, paranoia and anxiety were prevalent among survivors. These emotional responses escalated into conditions like PTSD.

The disaster had a profound effect on the belief systems of the people in Sirahan Village. They became more susceptible to unfounded fears and beliefs, such as trusting individuals claiming to predict future disasters. The Merapi disaster highlighted the need for psychological support in addition to material assistance. However, the delivery of psychological aid was often uncoordinated due to the influx of multiple aid providers.

In these difficult circumstances, hope intervention emerged as a potential psychological support method. Hope intervention involves goal setting, strategy planning and motivation enhancement. It can be administered in group sessions, fostering a sense of community and emotional support. Research indicated that hope intervention could effectively alleviate depression, increase agency thinking, enhance the meaningfulness of life and self-esteem, and reduce symptoms of depression and anxiety.

An open-access study from the Faculty of Psychology at Gadjah Mada University in Yogyakarta has carefully detailed how group-based hope intervention effectively reduced depression levels among survivors of the Mount Merapi cold lava flood in 2010. The research aimed to provide new insights into the application of positive psychology for survivors and benefit practitioners working with such populations. This research underscores the importance of addressing both the physical and psychological needs of disaster survivors, offering hope as a valuable tool for promoting emotional recovery.

Hope leads to luck

We often hear people say that someone is "lucky" or that they have had a "lucky break". Luck is a concept that has fascinated humanity for centuries. We often attribute success to luck, believing that some people are just born lucky, while others are not.

It is said that hope leads to luck, and there is truth to this notion. When we hold on to hope, when we nurture it and allow it to flourish, we open ourselves up to a world of abundance and possibility. Hope gives us the courage to take risks, push beyond our limits and believe that anything can be achieved. In short, hope is a mindset that enables us to make the most of what we have, rather than focusing on what we lack.

One of the ways in which hope creates luck is by increasing our resilience. Resilience is the ability to bounce back from setbacks and keep going in the face of adversity. In times of darkness and despair, when the weight of the world seems too heavy to bear, hope can seem like a distant dream. But it is precisely in these moments of darkness that hope transforms our lives, lifts us up and carries us towards the light. When we are hopeful, we are more likely to keep trying until we succeed. This resilience can lead to opportunities that we would not have otherwise had, as we continue to push forward even when things seem bleak.

When we embody hope, we become magnets for luck and good fortune. We attract positive energy and opportunities, and we begin to see the world in a new light. We are no longer limited by our fears or doubts but empowered by our belief in ourselves and in the limitless potential of the universe.

Tools for cultivating hope in times of crisis

"Hope is the heartbeat of the soul."—Michelle Horst

In times of great despair and hopelessness, it can be difficult to see any light at the end of the tunnel. Whether it is a personal crisis, a global pandemic or a natural disaster, the weight of the situation can feel unbearable. However, even in the darkest of moments, hope is not lost. There are strategies that you can adopt to find hope and keep pushing forward. Let me list some of these:

Acknowledge the pain

First and foremost, it is important to acknowledge the suffering that we are experiencing. Ignoring or suppressing these emotions will only lead to further distress. It is okay to grieve, to feel anger or sadness, to express these emotions in a healthy and constructive way. In fact, allowing ourselves to feel these emotions is a necessary step in the healing process.

Focus on the present moment

Dwelling on the problems of the past or worrying about the future only serves to increase anxiety and despair. It is easy to become overwhelmed by the enormity of our problems. But by taking a moment to ground ourselves in the present, we can regain our perspective. We need to centre ourselves in the here and now, and we can release the fear and anxiety that comes with worrying about the future. Mindfulness practices such as meditation or deep breathing are helpful in bringing our attention to the present moment and calming the mind.

Focus on the things that can be controlled

When life feels out of control, it is easy to spiral into hopelessness. However, by focusing on the things we can control, we can regain a sense of direction. Whether it is taking small steps towards a goal or establishing a routine, there are always actions we can take that can make a difference. We must remember that our circumstances are not permanent and that there is always the possibility that they'll change. We need to seize the moment and act on things we can control; this way we can create a sense of purpose.

Seek support

Irrespective of what a lot of people say or what sometimes our ego dictates, asking for help is actually a sign of strength and courage.

Reach out to those who care about us and are willing to offer their assistance. By sharing our struggles with others, we can gain new perspectives. Who knows, if we share a problem with a friend, they might share a solution from their own experience! Knowing that there are people who care about us and want to help will provide us comfort and reassurance, and we will be reminded that we are not alone.

Practise self-care

As I have discussed in multiple contexts in this book, we must take care of ourselves physically, emotionally and spiritually. This involves getting enough sleep, eating healthy foods, exercising and practising meditation. These activities help build resilience and we can find the strength to face our challenges with hope.

The story of Malala Yousafzai

In 1997, a young girl was born in the picturesque and lush Swat Valley of Pakistan. Named Malala by her parents, she grew up in a world of breath-taking natural beauty. But this world also held the constant threat of violence and oppression. In 2007, the Taliban took control of Swat Valley. The Taliban believe that girls should not be educated, and they began attacking schools and forcing girls to stay at home. However, Malala's family was passionate about education, and they believed that every child deserved the opportunity to learn and thrive.

Despite the danger and all the odds stacked against her, Malala had a fierce determination to learn and pursue her dreams. Not only did she continue to attend school, she also began advocating for girls' education and speaking out against the oppressive policies of the Taliban. Her courage and determination started getting noticed, and soon Malala became a powerful voice for change. She gave speeches, wrote articles and even started blogging for the BBC under a pseudonym, all for promoting education and equality.

Malala's bravery did not get unnoticed by the Taliban. In 2012, one morning when she was on her way to school, a masked gunman boarded her school bus and shot her in the head. The attack was an attempt to silence her and discourage other girls from speaking out. Malala, only fifteen years old at the time, was critically injured in the attack but miraculously survived. She was flown to a hospital in the United Kingdom for treatment where she had to undergo multiple surgeries and months of rehabilitation.

While she was recovering, Malala's story captured the attention of the world. She continued to speak out for education and women's rights, even addressing the United Nations in 2013, and went on to become the youngest ever Nobel Prize laureate at the age of seventeen a year later.

Despite the horrific attack, Malala remained hopeful and determined. She believed that education was the key to a brighter future—not just for herself, but for all children, especially girls. She has continued her advocacy work, founding the Malala Fund to promote education for girls around the world. Today, Malala is a global icon of hope and resilience, and her courage inspires people around the world. Her story reminds us that no matter how difficult the journey may be, there is always hope for a brighter tomorrow.

Hope can take many forms, it can be a small glimmer of light in a dark tunnel, or a raging fire that burns within us, driving us towards our goals. It can come from within, from a deep-seated belief in our abilities and our potential, or it can come from the people around us, who encourage us and believe in us even when we do not believe in ourselves.

Because the power of hope is unmatched, it can help us overcome the greatest of adversities and keep us going when all seems lost. Feeling hopeful is not just a state of mind; rather, it is a way of life, a force that can help us achieve our dreams and live a more fulfilling life. Fittingly, hope is what rounds up our exploration of the 8-H Principle.

Conclusion

In the midst of the fast-paced and interconnected modern world, there exists a pervasive sense of emptiness that we all grapple with. The relentless influx of news detailing wars and violence in today's world exerts profound pressure on our mental well-being. This unceasing barrage of negative information fosters an atmosphere of stress, leading to emotional exhaustion and a diminished capacity for empathy. At the same time, we witness an alarming increase in natural disasters, rising temperatures and ecosystem degradation. The loss of familiar landscapes and the threat to the planet's stability evoke a sense of grief and melancholy. The looming climate chaos amplifies feelings of uncertainty about the future, which takes an emotional toll on many of us. Add to this all, the problems closer home: societal pressures, the ever-present influence of social media, the pursuit of superficial success and the erosion of genuine human connections. This complex interplay of factors leads to a sense of void, leaving people yearning for something more profound and meaningful.

For me, facing the seriousness of death—as I recounted in the preface to this book—made me remember that survival is the most important thing for us. It is the foundation for our hopes, dreams and what we want to achieve. But just staying alive is not enough. We also need to have a reason for being here, a strong determination to make the world better: a purpose. Our purpose helps us know what direction to go in life and make choices that match our values and goals.

Moreover, it is through acts of generosity and selflessness that we authentically fulfil our life's purpose. Helping others, motivating them and crafting enduring beauty—these endeavours infuse our existence with meaning. Ultimately, what truly counts is not the span of years we traverse but the legacy we leave behind in the world.

Hence, within the abyss of emptiness that we often feel, there lies a glimmer of hope, a beacon that points towards the possibility of a brighter and more fulfilling future. The 8-H Principle is a set of guiding ideals that can steer each of us towards a purpose-driven life. It directs our attention to aspects that are pivotal to holistic welfare. With a comprehensive outlook on life, the 8-H Principle underscores the significance of persistence, empathy, self-nurturing and ingenuity. By embracing these values and integrating them into our daily routines, we can cultivate true human connections, attain success and leave a constructive impact on the world.

Life is the most precious gift we are given—a journey that we all embark on. It is a path that we all must walk, full of twists and turns, with no guarantee of what lies ahead. Each day is an opportunity to learn something new, to create something special and to leave behind a legacy that will continue to impact future generations.

Often, on this journey called life, we are so focused on achieving our goals that we forget to enjoy the journey or celebrate the little milestones we achieve every day. It is important to take the time to appreciate the little things along the way, the moments of joy, the lessons learned, and the people who have touched our lives.

Let us look at a little story.

Conclusion

In a quaint village nestled between rolling Himalayan hills and a glistening river, lived a man named Akash. In the village and beyond the valley, Akash was known for his honesty, humility and humaneness. He was an embodiment of these virtues, and his story inspired everyone around him.

Agriculture was the mainstay of these Himalayan villages, and Akash worked tirelessly as a farmer, tending to his land with utmost dedication. His days began with the rising sun, and he toiled under its golden rays, sowing seeds and nurturing the crops. His hard work was fuelled by a deep connection to the earth and a sincere desire to provide for his family and for the village. He never boasted about his labour or the bountiful harvests his fields produced. Instead, he always said that his success lay in the generosity of Nature and the support of his fellow villagers.

Amidst his busy routine, Akash embraced a unique hobby—sculpting. The river that galloped along the valley often brought with it pieces of wood. Akash would collect these pieces of driftwood and spend his evenings creating intricate sculptures from them. He sculpted wild and domestic animals, trees and other aspects of Nature. Akash never sought recognition for his artistic talents or made any effort to monetize them. Instead, he humbly shared his creations with others, hoping to bring a smile to their faces.

As the days turned into weeks and then months, a much-awaited event was on the horizon—the village's annual autumn holiday celebration. This holiday was a time for merriment, gratitude and unity. The villagers would gather, sharing stories, laughter and food. Akash eagerly looked forward to this holiday, as it was a time when the entire village came together as one big family.

However, fate had other plans. A sudden and mysterious illness struck Akash, leaving him bedridden and weak. The village was heartbroken, for Akash was not just a farmer, he was the heart and soul of their community. But Akash faced this challenge with the same qualities that defined him—honesty, humility and, most importantly, hope. He accepted the support and care of his fellow villagers with gratitude, recognizing that he was now on the receiving end of the humaneness he had always shown.

As the festive holiday drew near, the village decided to dedicate the celebration to Akash. They transformed his sculpting hobby into a collective project, creating a breath-taking sculpture that represented their love and appreciation. They worked tirelessly, mirroring the hard work Akash had put into his fields year after year. The celebration itself became a reflection of Akash's qualities—honesty in acknowledging his condition, humility in accepting help and hope that better days would come. And come they did.

With time, Akash's health improved and, even though still a bit weak, he was actually able to join the holiday celebration. The joy in his eyes and the tears in the villagers' eyes spoke volumes about the bond they shared. The sculpture stood tall, symbolizing the journey of a man who embodied the best of humanity.

Akash's story demonstrates that even in the face of challenges, honesty, humility and humanity could light the way. It emphasizes that hard work and hobbies balance life, while holidays remind us of the importance of unity and gratitude. Akash's journey is a testament to the power of these qualities we have called 8-H, showing that they could transform not just a man's life, but an entire community.

As we stand at the crossroads of our personal and collective journeys, we have the power to transform the void we often feel within us into a canvas of opportunity and growth. By channelling our energies into meaningful endeavours and nurturing our inner selves, we pave the way for a life filled with purpose. The future, even if it often looks bleak, holds the promise of a more connected and harmonious existence—a testament to the unwavering power of hope in shaping our destinies.